CHEFS OF DISTINCTION VOLUME THREE

Published in the United Kingdom by

Ptarmigan Publishing Ltd

46 New Park Street Devizes Wiltshire SN10 1DT

Telephone	+44 (0)1380 728700
Facsimile	+44 (0)1380 728701
E mail	enquiries@distinctionworld.com
Web site	**www.distinctionworld.com**

Publisher & managing director	Mark Hodson
Sales manager	Nick Holme
Production manager	Susan Parker
Administrator	Kate Mousley

Editing and page layout:

Mark Dawson

Colour origination and print:

Raithby, Lawrence & Company Ltd.

London and Leicester

© Ptarmigan Publishing Ltd 2002

ISBN 1 904122 05 1

British Library Cataloguing in Publication Data.

A catalogue record for this book is available from the British Library.

Front cover photograph:
Danesfield House Hotel & Spa

Title page photograph:
The Thatched Cottage Hotel & Restaurant

Back cover photograph:
City Cafe Restaurant, Bar & Terrace Bristol

CHEFS OF
DISTINCTION

VOLUME THREE

The King and I

CONTENTS

12

BAILIFFSCOURT HOTEL

DANIEL CLARKE

Seared scallops, parsnip purée,
honey, lime and bacon dressing

Roasted breast of duck, confit of leg,
fricassée of baby vegetables, orange sauce

Warm chocolate soufflé pudding,
roasted hazelnut and Baileys ice cream

17

BALLYNAHINCH CASTLE

ROBERT WEBSTER

Seared scallops, sweet peppers and soy oriental sauce

Pan fried halibut, baby asparagus, and saffron butter

Vanilla bavarois gateau,
marinated fruits and chocolate sauce

22

BLAKES HOTEL

NEVILLE CAMPBELL

Tortellini Landes foie gras

Baked sea bass with crispy fennel skin

Pandan pudding with blueberry compote

26

CITY CAFE RESTAURANT, BAR & TERRACE
BIRMINGHAM

MARTIN WALKER

Seared scallops with beetroot jam and bay infused sauce

Roast rack of Cornish lamb with black truffle potatoes

Lemon posset with blueberries and banana compote

31

CALLOW HALL

ANTHONY SPENCER

Sweet potato and butternut squash soup

Fillet of pork roasted in Parma ham with caramelised sage
and onion, crispy fried celeriac and sage and red wine jus

Raspberry and shortbread millefeuille with bittersweet
chocolate sorbet

36

CASHEL PALACE HOTEL

DECLAN HAYES

Seared king scallops, beetroot crème fraîche
and lemongrass velouté

Medallions of monkfish wrapped in smoked salmon
with a mushroom risotto and lime and honey vierge

Assiette au chocolat

42

CHARLTON HOUSE
& THE MULBERRY RESTAURANT

ADAM FELLOWS

Stuffed saddle of rabbit with mustard and herbs, honey
roast pork belly and fricassée of girolles and broad beans

Fillet of sea bass on basil crushed potato with aubergine
and courgette, black olive tapenade and sauce vierge

Chocolate and crème fraîche mousse,
exotic fruits and passion fruit sorbet

47

CHEWTON GLEN

PIERRE CHEVILLARD

Salad of duck and langoustine

Noisettes of lamb with a spaghetti of vegetables
and garlic and thyme jus

Summer pudding

52

CHILSTON PARK

GILES STONEHOUSE

Marinated red mullet with Provençal vegetables
and a cherry tomato vinaigrette

Roast lobster wrapped in pancetta
with a haricot bean and truffle fricassée

Summer pudding, passion fruit jelly,
and shortbread biscuit

58

CITY CAFE RESTAURANT, BAR & TERRACE
BRISTOL

GARY CLARKE

Slow roasted aubergine and Piedmontaise pepper
with fresh tortellini, red pepper dressing and pesto

Grilled halibut with cherry vine tomatoes, Kentish
asparagus, spring onions and coriander dressing

Vanilla crème brûlée with nut tuiles and chocolate sauce

64

DANESFIELD HOUSE HOTEL & SPA

DAMIAN BROOM

Ballottine of eel and horseradish, Tokay gelée

Blanquettes of veal belly with white truffle sauce

Warm pear tart with Stinking Bishop ice cream

SEAHAM HALL HOTEL & ORIENTAL SPA

JOHN CONNELL

Scottish langoustines with sweet spices
and a light fennel bavarois

Asian roasted seafood

SHARROW BAY

JUAN MARTIN/COLIN AKRIGG

Pan-fried scallops on roasted asparagus
with chive butter sauce

Roast quail on fondant potato
with wild mushroom and Madeira sauce

Dark chocolate parfait encased in a caramel box
with a raspberry sauce

SHEEN FALLS LODGE

CHRIS FARRELL

Ravioli of caramelised Autumn root vegetables,
plum tomato fondue, cappucino of bay leaf

Roast saddle of venison with braised cos, celeriac,
baby leek, and bitter chocolate sauce

Chocolate tuile barrel with marinated cherries
and fromage blanc mousse

SIMPSON'S RESTAURANT

LUKE TIPPING

Tronçonnettes of lobster, truffled spaghettini,
lobster & pepper sauce

Honey glazed shank of lamb, aubergine caviar,
lemon couscous with its own juice

Dome of strawberries in champagne jelly
with cheese ice cream

STUDLEY PRIORY HOTEL

SIMON CRANNAGE

Hot sphere of goat's cheese, red onion and port purée

Seared beef pavé, braised blade and horseradish faggot,
red wine glaze

Dark chocolate and banana fondant,
rum ice with Malibu jelly

THE SWAN HOTEL

SHAUN NAEN

Glazed asparagus with sauce Maltaise

Slow cooked veal belly

Iced sweet corn parfait and chocolate sorbet

THE SWAN AT STREATLEY

NEIL THRIFT

Seared seabass with Singapore noodles
and fresh langoustines

Tian of lamb with red wine butter sauce

Chocolate passion surprise

THE THATCHED COTTAGE
HOTEL & RESTAURANT

MARTIN MATYSIK

Lobster and avocado salad japonaise

Guinness marinated tenderloin of Angus beef
with basil mashed potatoes

Cappuccino ice-cream parfait

THE VINEYARD AT STOCKCROSS

JOHN CAMPBELL

Terrine of free range chicken and foie gras

Rabbit saddle, risotto of pea

Chocolate fondant

WINTERINGHAM FIELDS

GERMAIN SCHWAB

Foie gras terrine

Lovage pasta nest with Avruga caviar sauce

Fruit jellies

THE WORDSWORTH HOTEL

BERNARD WARNE

Assiette of duck

Roulade of chicken with spring onion, sunblush
tomatoes and feta cheese

Dark chocolate mousse with Griottine cherries

COMMITTED TO QUALITY

Talking with Peter Allen about his business is both inspiring and rather depressing. Inspiring, because his enthusiasm, knowledge, and passion come through with every utterance. Depressing, because one is rapidly made aware of how little respect the main operators in his field have for us, the consumers of their wares.

Peter's business is Aubrey Allen, supplier of premium quality meat, and among his most loyal customers are the chefs at some of the country's leading restaurants and hotels, perhaps the most demanding client base imaginable. Talk to any chef worthy of the title and he or she will confirm the simple truth that great cooking demands great ingredients. The reason for Aubrey Allen's success is straightforward: a constant emphasis on quality, delivered reliably at a fair price. As Peter himself expresses the equation: "I realised that butchers were divided into two camps. There was high quality at a high price, and low quality at a low price. What I set out to achieve

was high quality – the highest – at lower than premium prices. I'd learnt how to achieve volume sales from working with cheaper operators, and couldn't see any reason why the same methods shouldn't be applied to a quality product so I could keep margins lower."

Visiting Aubrey Allen's premises, incongruously tucked away in a light industrial area near the University of Warwick, demonstrates how this idea works in practice. To appreciate what sets his business apart, and revert to the depressing side of meeting Peter, one has first to understand the mechanics of preparing meat for consumption. The competitive demands of the market have led, through the basic laws of

economics, to the period between slaughter and packaging becoming shorter and shorter, leading to the present situation whereby the vast majority of the meat bought today has been vacuum-packed within twenty-four hours of slaughter. However, as any fine craftsman, dedicated vigneron, conscientious chef or master butcher will tell you, nothing worth having was ever created by the laws of economics alone. Meat treated in this way will still be saturated with blood; sealed into the packaging, this will effectively cause it to decompose. It is at this point that we can be grateful that it is generally eaten so soon after packaging, and draw a discreet veil over such other aspects as the inferior texture and lack of flavour to which so many of us have sadly become accustomed.

This haste is not only utterly detrimental to the quality of the product on our tables but, given the time – three years from conception to slaughter – and effort required to rear a beast, seems unseemly verging on the obscene. It is all too easy to see how farmers might be tempted to discard the good practices that historically

have elevated our produce into the highest ranks and learned to cut their own corners. After all, if quality is no longer a factor in the end product, why bother with quality of husbandry?

To mature properly, meat requires up to three weeks on the bone. All Aubrey Allen meats are matured in this way, dry cured in the Warwickshire cold stores. The difference? Let Peter elucidate – without deviation or hesitation – taking as his subject a properly prepared steak: "There are three tastes. There's the crust, which gives you the chef's input. There's the explosion of succulence in the mouth. Finally there's the aftertaste, the lingering flavours sealed in by the maturing process. And there's no short cut to that result. Of course you can get cheaper meat than ours: every day you'll drive past pubs offering a 12oz steak for £5.95. But it's just like wine. You can buy a bottle for £2.99, but you'd be a damned fool if you expected it to bear comparison with a cru classé. Our job is to support the restaurant and enhance its reputation by guaranteeing the quality of the produce the chef uses."

The comparison with wine is helpful in another, even more critical sense. Wine denomination systems such as the French Appellation Contrôlée work because they reassure the customer. They guarantee that the end product has been made by approved methods from permitted ingredients in a designated area, and that the wine has been assessed by experts as conforming to an established quality standard. The Aubrey Allen Assured marque provides the same reassurance. A customer buying meat with this endorsement not only knows that the meat will have been properly prepared, but that it has been sourced from carefully selected and regularly vetted suppliers who share the same dedication to quality.

Every carcass that enters Peter's premises is tagged for provenance. The label on a side of beef hanging in the store showed not only that it originated from the Duke of Buccleuch's herds but also the name of the farmer, the weight at slaughter, the date and time of slaughter, and the category of meat by fat content and shape. Bob, master of the meat rooms that are the heart of the operation, guided me through the basics of this assessment, sparing no contempt for those lesser beasts whose badly brought up bodies would never be permitted to darken his doors. His conclusion; "breeding, grass, and water: it's as simple as that". Simple, but not easily come by. Peter only buys the best: beef from Scotland, lamb from Cornwall, pork from Lincolnshire, chickens from the Loire. "These producers can sell their meat anywhere and I've worked hard building up a relationship over 25 years to make sure they sell it to us. I go to Scotland, Cornwall, and France regularly because I have to know they're doing the job properly."

The average age of a chicken sold in the British high street is six weeks and two days. It used to be eight weeks, but genetic engineering and chemical tinkering has improved the profitability, if not the quality of life, of the birds by almost 25%. By comparison the chickens Peter buys from his French farmers are rank amateurs, allowed to roam free for between eighteen and twenty two weeks and feeding on natural corn. But again it's the time factor that is critical. The real secret of the flavour is that they are more mature, two and a half times older than an ordinary commercial chicken. And, as Peter says, "taste like chicken used to taste".

The end result of this commitment to quality is that meat bearing the Aubrey Allen Assured marque now goes out to over 75% of the top chefs in the Midlands, with between 60 and 70 courier deliveries a day to others as far away as Padstow (guess who). And with Aubrey Allen Direct, the general public can now get in on the act. This home delivery mail order service provides not only Aubrey Allen's prime cuts of beef, lamb and pork but the poultry, game, farm cured bacon, black pudding, and a menu of 17 sausages all made with natural ingredients and real herbs and spices hitherto available only to professional kitchens. The success of this venture has convinced Peter that his passion for genuine meat is met by a similar desire for quality among a significant number of us: "the number of people who care about quality meat is still small, but it's slowly rising".

Buying for quality has sometimes seemed an alien concept in the UK. Peter contrasts the British attitude with that of France, where shoppers have always happily paid a higher price for a chicken that meets their demands. But in recent times a number of factors have brought about a resurgence of interest in food standards. Ironically, among the most important of these are the scandals that have all too regularly beset a food industry in which already lax standards have routinely been abused. Asked about the BSE crisis, Peter

asserts "Pretty ghastly, but I have to say it helped us enormously. For once the focus was firmly on quality, and that's the arena in which we want to compete and know we can win. Because of it, people are now thinking very hard about where meat comes from and how it's treated. As long as there are discerning chefs and a public with good taste, I'll have a good business." Out of respect for ourselves, and also I believe for the animals we eat, we have a duty to ensure that Aubrey Allen and others like them continue to prosper.

Contact: Alan Healy
Aubrey Allen Limited
Curriers Close, Canley, Coventry CV4 8AW

Tel: 02476 422 222 Fax: 02476 421 555
Email: alan@aubreyallen.co.uk
Web: www.aubreyallen.co.uk

BAILIFFSCOURT HOTEL

Daniel Clarke

Seared scallops, parsnip purée, honey, lime and bacon dressing

Serves 4

Ingredients:

12 diver caught scallops

Olive oil

Lemon juice

For the parsnip purée:

4 large parsnips

250ml milk

250ml water

50g butter

For the dressing:

1 tablespoon honey

1 tablespoon fresh lime juice

1 tablespoon sherry vinegar

3 tablespoons olive oil

$^1/_2$ teaspoon chopped ginger

1 tablespoon bacon, roasted and diced

To prepare the purée, peel the parsnips and chop them up into small even pieces, then place them in a pan with the milk, water and butter and bring to the boil. Simmer until tender; this should take twenty to twenty-five minutes. Strain and leave the parsnips to cool for around half an hour, then blend until smooth. Check the seasoning, and if necessary push through a sieve.

For the dressing, mix together all the ingredients and whisk vigorously for two minutes.

Finally, heat a little olive oil in a pan, then cook the scallops for one minute on one side. Turn the scallops and take the pan off the heat, then season with salt and lemon juice. Set aside for a short while to rest before serving.

Roasted breast of duck, confit of leg, fricassée of baby vegetables, orange sauce

Serves 4

Ingredients:

4 x 175/200g duck breasts, Magret or Challon

3 baby leeks, blanched

3 baby carrots, blanched

3 baby onions

1 tablespoon broad beans, blanched

Olive oil

For the confit:

2 large duck legs

1 litre duck fat

1 clove garlic, chopped

Zest and juice of 1 orange

120ml balsamic vinegar

120ml hazelnut oil

2 shallots, finely chopped

For the sauce:

1 litre freshly squeezed orange juice

2 shallots, finely chopped

1 litre duck or chicken stock

To prepare the confit, rub the duck legs with garlic and salt, then leave for twelve hours. Wash off the salt and dry. Bring the duck fat to the boil in a heavy based pan, then add the duck legs and place in the oven for four hours at 175°C. Remove from the oven and place the legs on a tray to cool, then take off the bone and shred the meat. While the meat is cooling, bring the orange zest and juice, balsamic vinegar, hazelnut oil and shallots to the boil in a saucepan, simmering for ten minutes. Mix in the shredded meat, then pour the mixture into moulds and set aside to cool.

For the sauce, heat all the ingredients in a saucepan, reduce by half, then pass through a chinois and set aside.

Cook the duck breasts skin side down for six minutes on a medium heat, then turn and continue cooking for a further two minutes. Place the breasts on a tray in a 180°C oven for two minutes, then remove, season, and leave to rest for ten minutes. Bring a pan of water to the boil, add salt and a little butter, and cook the baby vegetables for around a minute until tender: place the vegetables on a tray and season with salt.

Slice the duck breasts and place on the plate with the confit: arrange the vegetables and finish with the orange sauce.

Warm chocolate soufflé pudding, roasted hazelnut and Baileys ice cream

10 portions

For the soufflé pudding:

6 eggs, separated

110g dark chocolate

110g ground almonds

50g breadcrumbs

110g caster sugar

Whisk the egg yolks and half the sugar in a blender for eight minutes until it is thick and glossy. Gently melt the chocolate and fold into the mixture. Whisk the egg whites with the rest of the sugar; when stiffened, add to the chocolate mix, carefully folding it in. Just as carefully fold in the almonds and breadcrumbs until they are fully incorporated, then spoon into buttered 9cm pudding basins. Cook in a bain marie for 12 to 14 minutes at 150°C, then leave to cool for five minutes and turn out.

For the ice cream:

10 egg yolks

220g caster sugar

2 vanilla pods, deseeded

700ml whipping cream

240ml Baileys liqueur

110g hazelnuts, roasted

Whisk the egg yolks for five minutes, meanwhile boil the sugar with a little water for five minutes, then add to the yolks and whisk until cold. Add the vanilla and set aside. Add the cream and Baileys to the ice cream base and churn in an ice cream machine until set: when the churning is almost complete, add the hazelnuts.

BALLYNAHINCH CASTLE

Robert Webster

Seared scallops, sweet peppers and soy oriental sauce

Serves 4

Ingredients:

16 medium scallops, cleaned

4 yellow peppers

4 red peppers

160ml olive oil

300g mashed potato

To garnish:

1 aubergine

16 sprigs chervil

For the sauce:

100ml tomato ketchup

3 teaspoons sweet soy sauce

5 teaspoons oyster sauce

1 teaspoon chopped ginger

1 dessert spoon chopped leaf coriander

Prepare the sauce in advance by mixing together all the ingredients, then set aside in a cool place.

Halve the peppers and remove the seeds, then set out on a roasting tray, cover with oil, and roast until soft. Put the roasted peppers in a plastic bag, tied at the top, and leave to cool. When they are cold the skins should come off easily; once skinned, chop and store until required.

Sauté the scallops in a hot pan for about two minutes each side; meanwhile place a portion of seasoned mashed potato on each plate. Put the scallops on the mash, arranging the peppers and chervil around and decorating as required with the sauce.

Pan fried halibut, baby asparagus, and saffron butter

Serves 4

Ingredients:

4 x 225g halibut fillets

28 spears baby asparagus

2 tablespoons olive oil

*16 new or château potatoes
for garnish*

For the saffron vinaigrette:

140g unsalted butter

150ml dry white wine

1 shallot, finely chopped

Pinch of saffron threads

150ml fish stock

*2 tomatoes,
peeled, sliced, and chopped*

2 sprigs fresh tarragon

To make the vinaigrette, clarify the butter by bringing it to a simmer in a small pan, skimming off any froth from the surface. When the surface has cleared let the butter settle. Pour off the butter, leaving the watery, milky liquid in the pan. Discard the liquid and keep the butter.

Bring the shallots and wine to a simmer in a small pan, then add the fish stock and saffron and simmer again until it has reduced by a third. Season with salt and pepper, add the tomatoes, tarragon and clarified butter, and keep warm until needed.

Trim 5mm from the bottom of each stalk and blanch the asparagus in salted boiling water by bringing the water back to the boil after insertion then taking the pan off the heat and under cold running water until the asparagus is cold. Set aside.

Heat the olive oil in a good sized heavy based frying pan. When the oil is hot, season the fillets of fish and place them carefully in the pan; if the pan is hot enough the halibut won't stick. Cook over a medium heat for three minutes without moving, then turn the fillets on their sides and cook for a further two minutes. Repeat with the other side of the fillet; by which time the fish will be ready.

Remove the portions from the pan and place on warm plates. Add the asparagus to the pan and sauté for one minute, then arrange the spears on top of the fish. Drizzle saffron vinaigrette around the plate and serve at once with the warmed château or new potatoes.

PETER BRAZIL: SOUS CHEF

Vanilla bavarois gateau, marinated fruits and chocolate sauce

Serves 5

Almond sponge:

40g icing sugar

40g ground almonds

10g flour

1 tablespoon melted butter

1 egg yolk

2 egg whites

Whip the egg whites and mix a quarter of the whip with all the other ingredients in a bowl. Fold in the remainder of the egg whites, then gently spread the mix in a thin layer over an oven mat. Bake for seven minutes at 230°C.

Chocolate sauce:

60g cocoa powder

60g caster sugar

200ml double cream

50g butter

Melt the butter in a saucepan, then add the other ingredients and bring to the boil for about three minutes.

Marinated fruits:

$^1/_4$ of a green apple

$^1/_2$ a kiwi fruit

$^1/_4$ of a nectarine

50g pineapple

80g strawberries

Juice of half a lemon

Pinch chopped lime zest

Dice the fruits to approximately 3mm cubes, then place all except the strawberries in a bowl with the lemon juice and lime zest. Leave in the fridge for 40 minutes, stirring gently every ten minutes or so. Add the diced strawberries just before serving.

Vanilla bavarois:

125ml fresh double cream

125ml milk

1 vanilla pod

4 egg yolks

50g sugar

8g gelatine

125ml whipped cream

Make a crème anglaise by bringing the double cream, milk and vanilla pod to the boil, then adding the egg yolks and sugar. Heat the milk mix gently for a few seconds without letting it return to the boil, then add the gelatine softened in cold water. When the anglaise is cold and set, add a quarter of the whipped cream, then fold in the rest.

Take five moulds 8cm in diameter by 5cm deep. From the sponge, cut out five strips 24 x 2.5 cm and five discs 7cm in diameter. Line the moulds with the strips, smooth side against the mould wall, and insert the discs at the base of the moulds. Fill with the bavarois and leave in the fridge for at least an hour.

CEDRIC BOTTARLINI: PASTRY CHEF

BLAKES HOTEL

Neville Campbell

Tortellini Landes foie gras

serves 4

Ingredients:

100g foie gras trimmings

25g shallots, chopped

25g wild mushrooms, chopped

1 small truffle, finely diced

1 packet wonton wrappers

1 egg, beaten

4 slices raw foie gras

For the prune jus:

500ml veal stock or quality beef stock

250g prunes, plus 8 for garnish

1 glass red wine

For the beurre blanc

1 glass white wine

3 large shallots, finely chopped

3 sprigs thyme

*200g chilled unsalted butter,
cut into small cubes,
plus extra for frying the mushrooms*

75g wild mushrooms

Chopped fresh chives

To make the tortellini, mix together the foie gras trimmings, shallots, wild mushrooms and truffle and season with salt and pepper. Brush the wonton wrappers with beaten egg (this will seal the filling in), then place a small amount of the filling in the centre of each one. Fold the wrapper into a semi-circle, pull in the tips until both ends meet and then press them together. Chill until needed

To make the prune jus, put the stock, prunes and red wine in a pan and simmer until reduced to a fairly syrupy consistency. Pass through a fine sieve, pushing with the back of a ladle so some of the prune pulp goes through, and then set aside.

To make the beurre blanc, put the wine, shallots and thyme into a pan and simmer until the wine has reduced to a glaze. Whisk in the butter a few pieces at a time until it emulsifies and then strain the sauce into a clean pan. Season to taste.

Cook the tortellini in lightly salted boiling water, then drain well. In a little butter, quickly sauté the wild mushrooms for the beurre blanc until tender, seasoning with salt and pepper. In a separate pan, sauté the foie gras for 30 seconds on each side. Heat the prunes and keep warm.

Place the foie gras slices in the centre of each serving plate, place the prunes on top and then arrange the tortellini around the foie gras. Coat the tortellini with the prune jus. Add the sautéed mushrooms to the beurre blanc and bring to the boil carefully. Add the chives and spoon the sauce over the tortellini.

Baked sea bass with crispy fennel skin

serves 4

Ingredients:

1 large shallot, chopped

Pinch of saffron

175ml white wine

250ml fish stock

100ml double cream

4 x 175g sea bass fillets

Oil for deep-frying

25g fennel seeds, crushed

5g rock salt

*Pinch of yukari seasoning
(available from Japanese shops)*

Pinch of Cayenne pepper

Olive oil

For the braised fennel

*1 fennel bulb,
cut into batons 4mm thick*

200ml chicken stock

Knob of butter

Put the shallot, saffron, white wine and fish stock in a pan and boil until reduced by half, then add the cream and reduce by half again. Set aside.

For the braised fennel, put the fennel into a pan, half cover with stock, then add the butter and some salt and pepper. Cover and braise until tender.

To make the crispy fennel skin, skin the sea bass fillets and set the fillets aside. Remove the scales from the skin, blanch it in a pan of boiling water for 2 seconds, then plunge it into ice-cold water. Drain well. Pat the skin dry with a cloth, cut it into rectangles and deep-fry in hot oil until crisp. Drain well and flatten gently to obtain a perfect shape; trim with scissors. Coat with the crushed fennel seeds and rock salt and then garnish with diagonal strips of yukari seasoning and cayenne pepper.

Sauté the fish briefly in a little olive oil until golden brown on both sides, then transfer it to an oven preheated to 220°C to finish cooking. Meanwhile, reheat the sauce and the braised fennel.

To serve, place the braised fennel on each plate, put the fish on top and then put the crispy skin on top of the fish. Pour the sauce around the plate.

Pandan pudding with blueberry compote

serves 4

Ingredients:

*40g fresh pandan leaves
(available from Thai and Malaysian
shops), chopped*

200ml skimmed milk

200ml double cream

Zest of 1 orange

Zest of 1 lemon

1 vanilla pod

6 eggs, separated

100g caster sugar

2 gelatine leaves

For the blueberry compote:

350g blueberries

50g caster sugar

$^1/_4$ cinnamon stick

$^1/_4$ fresh red chilli

Liquidise the pandan leaves and milk until they become a rich green colour. Put the mixture into a pan with the cream and the orange and lemon zest. Split the vanilla pod open and scrape out the seeds, then add the pod and seeds to the pan and bring to the boil. Meanwhile, mix together the egg yolks and half the sugar in a bowl. Pour the pandan mixture on to the yolks, stirring all the time, then return to the pan and cook, stirring constantly, until the mixture has thickened enough to coat the back of the spoon. Remove from the heat. Soak the gelatine leaves in cold water for 5 minutes, then drain well and stir into the custard until dissolved. Pass the mixture through a fine sieve and cool rapidly.

Whisk the egg whites to soft peaks and fold in the remaining sugar. Fold the egg whites into the custard when it is nearly cold, then spoon the mixture into 4 square lined moulds and leave in the fridge to set.

Meanwhile, make the blueberry compote. Heat 250g of the blueberries in a pan with the sugar and a dash of water until the sugar has dissolved, then blitz to a purée in a blender. Add the cinnamon, chilli and remaining blueberries and leave to cool.

To serve, turn out the puddings on to 4 plates. Hollow out a square hole about 5mm deep in each one. Arrange the blueberries from the compote in lines in the holes, then pour in enough of the liquid so that the blueberries are almost covered. Serve with the remaining compote.

CITY CAFE RESTAURANT, BAR & TERRACE

BIRMINGHAM

Martin Walker

Seared scallops with beetroot jam and bay infused sauce

Serves 4

Ingredients:

12 scallops

40g dandelion leaves

Half a lemon

Sunflower oil

For the bay sauce:

2 shallots, peeled and chopped

1 small clove garlic

6 bay leaves

6 black peppercorns

50ml white wine

25g butter

150ml double cream

For the beetroot jam:

1kg cooked beetroot, diced

100g light brown sugar

Zest of half a lemon

Zest of half an orange

2 bay leaves

300ml water

To make the beetroot jam, place all the ingredients in a heavy bottomed pan and cook slowly for one and a half hours, then blend in a processor until smooth.

For the bay sauce, sweat the shallots and garlic in the butter until soft, then add the peppercorns and bay leaves and continue cooking for one minute. Add the wine and reduce by half, then add the cream and reduce until the sauce coats the back of a spoon. Strain the liquid into a clean pan and keep warm.

To serve, heat a frying pan and thinly coat with sunflower oil; brush the scallops with soft butter and sear one side quickly for one minute. Turn, squeeze over the lemon juice, and remove to keep warm. Pour sauce onto warm plates with a quenelle of jam on the edge, and arrange the scallops with a few dandelion leaves.

Roast rack of Cornish lamb with black truffle potatoes

Serves 4

Ingredients:

4 x 3-bone racks of Cornish lamb

For the jus:

*Mirepoix of 1 carrot,
1 stick of celery, 1 leek*

2 litres veal stock

10g thyme, chopped

*2 tomatoes,
skinned, deseeded and diced*

500g lamb trimmings

Small glass red wine

Small glass Madeira

For the potatoes:

8 black truffle potatoes

8 ratte potatoes

1 shallot, finely chopped

12 chives, finely chopped

25ml extra virgin olive oil

240g baby spinach

Prepare the jus by reducing the veal stock by half; meanwhile, caramelise the lamb trimmings, thyme, and mirepoix in a large pan, add the Madeira and wine, and reduce by half. Pour in the veal stock and continue to reduce until coating consistency, then strain into a clean pan and keep hot.

Boil the potatoes for 15 minutes, then strain. When they have slightly cooled slice lengthwise to a thickness of about 5mm, then set aside.

Roast the lamb in a 200°C oven to the desired degree, then leave to rest: medium takes 20 – 30 minutes. While the meat is roasting heat the oil in a frying pan, add and lightly brown the shallots, then put in the potatoes to reheat and add the chives. In a separate pan, quickly cook the baby spinach seasoned with salt and pepper until the leaves have wilted.

To serve arrange the potatoes in a ring on hot plates, with the baby spinach above the potatoes. Sit the lamb on the spinach and pour sauce around the plate.

Lemon posset with blueberries and banana compote

Serves 4

Posset, which originated in the middle ages as a curdled milk drink, has evolved into this smooth mousse-like dessert.

Bring the cream, caster sugar and lemon zest to the boil, then remove from the heat and add the lemon juice: pass the liquid through a fine strainer. Dice the banana and toss the chunks in lemon juice mixed with a little icing sugar. Gently cook the blueberries with the sugar for a couple of minutes.

Serve in margarita glasses: place a spoon of diced banana in the base, then a layer of blueberries, finally pouring over the posset mix. Decorate with a slice of banana and a sprig of mint.

Ingredients:

450g double cream

120g caster sugar

Zest of 1 lemon

Juice of 3 lemons

1 banana, diced
(keep 4 slices for decoration)

1 punnet blueberries

1¹/₂ teaspoons sugar

Icing sugar

4 sprigs mint

CALLOW HALL

Anthony Spencer

Sweet potato and butternut squash soup

Serves 4

Ingredients:

25g butter

25g flour (optional)

*2 orange sweet potatoes
(apprx 250g peeled and diced)*

*1 butternut squash (apprx 250g
peeled, deseeded, and diced)*

*1 medium onion
(apprx 150g peeled and sliced)*

1 bouquet garni

1 bay leaf

1 litre light vegetable stock

250ml single cream

To garnish:

Swirl of cream

Coriander leaves

Sweat the onions, sweat potato, and butternut squash in the butter: for a thicker soup add flour at this point to make a roux, although natural thickening will come from the sweet potato. Add the stock, bouquet garni and bay leaf, season lightly, bring to the boil and simmer for 30 minutes; longer for a thicker consistency. Remove the bouquet garni and bay leaves and add the cream, blending until smooth. Check the seasoning; add a swirl of cream and a few coriander leaves for decoration when serving.

Fillet of pork roasted in Parma ham with caramelised sage and onion, crispy fried celeriac and sage and red wine jus

Serves 4

Ingredients:

2 large pork fillets, trimmed

8 slices Parma ham, thinly sliced

3 cloves garlic, crushed

1 bunch fresh sage

3 tablespoons olive oil

2 large onions, sliced

1 small firm celeriac, finely sliced

For the sauce:

2 litres good beef stock

375ml red wine

2 dessert spoons redcurrant jelly

25g butter

1 large onion

40g caster sugar

2 teaspoons finely chopped sage

Blend the garlic, olive oil and a handful of sage leaves into a paste. Lay four slices of Parma ham on a length of cling film and spread with the paste, then lay one of the pork fillets across the ham and season with freshly ground black pepper. Roll the pork tightly in the ham (making sure the film doesn't get caught in the roll) and repeat the process with the other fillet. Remove the cling film and roast in a 200°C oven for 15 to 20 minutes (12 minutes if fan assisted). Meanwhile, in a thick bottomed frying pan cook the two sliced onions until dark brown, adding sage and seasoning.

For the sauce add the wine to the beef stock in a pan, bring to the boil and reduce: at the same time cook the onion to a deep brown over a moderate heat, then turn up the heat and add sugar until the onions caramelise. Add to the reducing stock and wine, then add the redcurrant jelly, butter, and a little salt and pepper. Continue to reduce until roughly half a litre of sauce remains, then strain through a fine sieve and add the chopped sage.

Deep fry the shredded celeriac until golden brown, dry off the fat on absorbent kitchen paper and lightly salt. To serve place thick slices of pork fillet around the onions and pour sauce around. Arrange the fried celeriac on top and garnish with sage leaves.

Raspberry and shortbread millefeuille with bittersweet chocolate sorbet

Serves 6

Shortbread:

(makes sufficient to keep 1 chef happy for apprx 1 week)

750g flour

400g butter, slightly salted

250g caster sugar

2 small eggs

7.5cm diameter cutter

Beat the sugar and butter together until creamy, then mix in the eggs, followed by the flour. Roll out the dough to around a third of an inch in thickness and cut out discs with the cutter. Bake at just under 150°C on greaseproof paper and leave on the tray to cool.

Raspberry filling and coulis:

4 punnets raspberries

Juice and zest of 1 lemon

110g sugar

200ml whipped cream

Icing sugar for dusting

To make the coulis, gently simmer two punnets of the raspberries with the lemon juice, zest, and sugar. Blend and finely strain.

The remaining raspberries are layered with cream and shortbread biscuit into millefeuille stacks and dusted with icing sugar.

For the sorbet:

150g bittersweet chocolate, at least 53.5% cacao

1 vanilla pod, split

1 pint water

75g granulated sugar

15g unsweetened cocoa powder

Finely chop the chocolate. Scrape out the vanilla seeds and place in a saucepan with the water, sugar, cocoa powder and pod. Bring to the boil, then add the chopped chocolate, whisking continually to combine the mixture. As soon as the liquid comes to the boil, remove from the heat and rapidly cool on a bain marie of cold water. Extract the vanilla pod, and when the liquid is cold either freeze in an ice cream machine or place the bowl in the freezer, periodically stirring until set. Remove from the freezer ten minutes before serving to allow to soften a little.

To serve, drizzle a zigzag of coulis on the plate with a shortbread stack on one side and a scoop of sorbet on the other.

CASHEL PALACE

Declan Hayes

Seared king scallops, beetroot crème fraîche and lemongrass velouté

Serves 4

Ingredients:

16 king scallops, washed and dried

16 slices cooked fresh beetroot

200ml crème fraîche

1 wedge of lemon

For the sauce:

25g shallots

25g carrots

24g leeks (white part only)

50g lemon grass

150g butter

200ml cognac

1 litre fish stock

250ml double cream

25g cold butter

2 bay leaves

10g chives

To garnish:

Deep fried leek, diced

Julienne of beetroot

Chopped chives

Blend four of the beetroot slices together with the lemon juice and crème fraîche, then leave to one side.

To prepare the sauce, finely dice the vegetables and sweat in the butter for five minutes. Deglaze the pan with the cognac and reduce the liquid by half, then add the fish stock, lemon grass and bay leaves. Simmer for twenty minutes then pass through a fine strainer, keeping the strained vegetables. In a clean pan reduce the strained stock by half, then add the double cream and simmer until the liquid coats the back of a spoon: finish by whisking in the cold butter then leave to one side. Return the vegetables to the sauce before serving.

Toss the washed and drained scallops in olive oil and gently sear each side for thirty seconds then season. Gently sear the remaining beetroot slices until crisp.

To serve place three beetroot slices on each plate, then place a scallop on top of each, with the fourth scallop on top. Place three teaspoons of the crème fraîche on each plate, then gently ladle the velouté around the plate. Finally, garnish each scallop with the julienne of beetroot and leek, lightly sprinkling the top of each with chopped chives.

Medallions of monkfish wrapped in smoked salmon with a mushroom risotto and lime and honey vierge

Serves 4

For the risotto:

250g risotto rice

*150g wild mushrooms
(eg cèpe, shiitaki, oyster)*

25g butter

25ml olive oil

2 bay leaves

Sprig of thyme

50g grated Parmesan

15g garlic, chopped

2 plum tomatoes, finely diced

1 litre fish stock

75ml white wine

For the monkfish:

4 x 150g monkfish fillets

8 slices smoked salmon

50g butter

20ml olive oil

Juice of half a lemon

For the sauce:

50g shallots, sliced

50g spring onions

50g onion, diced

50g thyme

50g tomato, finely diced

200ml olive oil

30ml honey

75ml white wine

Juice of half a lime

For the risotto, melt the butter and olive oil in a thick-bottom pan, then add the risotto rice and stir until the rice is completely coated. Add the herbs, bay leaf, garlic, and wild mushrooms, then deglaze the pan with the wine and reduce the liquid by half. Slowly add the fish stock, one ladleful at a time, allowing the rice to absorb each one: when this is complete, leave on one side to rest. Stir in the Parmesan and diced tomato immediately before serving.

To prepare the monkfish, cut each fillet into three medallions of around 50g. Wrap each medallion in smoked salmon, brush with olive oil then gently sear for thirty seconds on both sides in the butter and lemon juice seasoned with salt and pepper. Finish cooking in the oven for ten minutes at 180°C.

For the sauce, lightly sauté the onions and shallots and add the herbs. Add the lime juice, then deglaze with the wine, add the olive oil, blanched spring onions and tomato, and leave to one side to infuse. Serve slightly warm.

To serve place three one-inch ringlets of risotto around the plate at different heights, with a piece of monkfish on each. Dress the plate with the vierge sauce, with a garnish of chopped spring onion on each monkfish piece to finish.

Assiette au chocolat

Serves 12

Chocolate hazelnut parfait:

250g egg yolks

225g sugar

75g water

100g hazelnuts

135g cocoa powder

125g dark chocolate

1 litre whipping cream

Beat the egg yolks in a mixer, then boil the sugar and water together to 120°C, then pour over the yolks and beat until cold. Meanwhile, roast the hazelnuts in the oven for ten minutes at 170°C then pulverise in a processor until finely ground. Gently melt the cocoa powder and chocolate together over a bain marie, then pour over the yolk mixture with the hazelnuts and whisk together. Separately whisk the cream to a soft peak, then fold into the mix. Pour the completed parfait into pyramid moulds and place in the freezer to set.

Orange truffle parcel:

120ml egg whites
150g sugar
15g cornflour
110g almonds

Make a Japanese meringue by beating the egg whites until stiff, gradually adding the sugar as you go. Fold in the cornflour and almonds, then bake at 150°C for 30 minutes until golden brown and dry. Cool.

95g almonds
95g icing sugar
60ml stock syrup
2 egg whites
12 egg yolks
85g caster sugar
1 teaspoon vanilla essence
115g flour
85g cocoa powder

For the chocolate sponge, blend the almonds, icing sugar and stock syrup together to make a paste, then add the egg whites. Whisk the yolks, caster sugar, and vanilla essence to ribbon stage, then add to the almond mix. Sift together the flour and cocoa powder, and fold into the sponge mix: spread to about 1cm depth and bake on a sheet pan for eight minutes at 220°C.

300ml double cream
350ml Grand Marnier
450g dark chocolate

Prepare the ganache by boiling the cream with 30ml of the Grand Marnier; pour the hot liquid over the chocolate, beating until all the chocolate has melted.

Cut the sponge in two and place one of the halves on a tray: sprinkle with Grand Marnier. Cover the sponge with a layer of ganache, then a layer of Japanese meringue. Repeat the process: another layer of sponge sprinkled with Grand Marnier, another layer of ganache, with a final topping of meringue. Put the tray in the fridge to set, then cut into squares.

For the parcels, melt couverture chocolate to 49°C, then pour out 3/4 of the mix and spread with a palate knife until it cools to 26°. Return the cooled portion to the remaining chocolate and blend: this should bring the melted chocolate to the ideal temperature of 32°. Measure and cut out sheets of plastic – sandwich bags or similar – the right size to wrap up the squares, then lay the plastic out flat and spread with chocolate. Re-wrap the squares, removing the plastic when the chocolate has set hard to create the chocolate 'parcel'.

Chocolate and raspberry mousse teardrop:

2 egg whites
5 egg yolks
150g sugar
50ml water
250g dark chocolate
300g whipping cream

120ml double cream
25g butter
100g dark chocolate

Make teardrop shapes using card or acetate and cover with tempered chocolate, using the coated plastic method outlined for the Orange truffle parcel: line the chocolate teardrops with fresh raspberries. Whisk together the egg yolks and whites; at the same time boil the sugar and water together to 120°C, then pour the syrup over the whisked egg mixture and beat until cold. Melt 250g of the chocolate and fold into the mix: finally, fold in the whipped cream and pour into the moulds.

Finish the teardrop by boiling the cream and butter together then stirring in the 100g of chocolate: when the glaze has cooled slightly, pour over the top of the teardrops.

Assemble all three elements on a plate, decorating with raspberry coulis, chocolate ganache and mint leaves.

CHARLTON HOUSE & THE MULBERRY RESTAURANT

Adam Fellows

Stuffed saddle of rabbit with mustard and herbs, honey roast pork belly and fricassée of girolles and broad beans

Serves 4

Ingredients:

2 rabbit saddles

150g pork belly (smoked)

2 large tablespoons honey

40g broad beans

2 tomatoes

1 tablespoon flat parsley, chopped

120g girolles

100ml white wine

100ml white wine vinegar

10 coriander seeds

1 tablespoon sugar

2 shallots

100ml vegetable oil

100ml olive oil

For the herb crust: ·

2 slices white bread, dried

40g fresh mixed herbs

2 tablespoons wholegrain mustard

Bone the rabbit saddles intact and cut in half lengthways. Place the bread in a food processor and process to fine breadcrumbs, then add the herbs and continue processing until a dark green colour is achieved. Spread the mustard over the rabbit pieces and sprinkle with the herb breadcrumbs, then roll up and string each of the saddles. Roast in an oven at 180°C for eight minutes, then leave to rest.

Poach the pork belly in gently boiling water for one and a half hours until soft, then leave to cool. Smear with the honey and roast for around 15 minutes at 200°C until the honey is starting to caramelise.

Clean and quickly wash the girolles. Chop the shallots finely and place in a pan with the wine, vinegar, and sugar; reduce the mixture by half. Add both the oils and cook for a further ten minutes, then pour the liquid over the girolles and leave for at least two hours. Blanch the broad beans and remove from their pods and peel and dice the tomatoes.

To serve, cut the pork belly into 5mm slices and fry on both sides. Warm the girolles in a pan with the broad beans, tomato dice and parsley leaves. Cut the rabbit saddles in half lengthways: put the broad beans and girolles on the plate, with the rabbit above and the pork belly on top.

Fillet of sea bass on basil crushed potato with aubergine and courgette, black olive tapenade and sauce vierge

Serves 4

Ingredients:

4 x 180g fillets sea bass

2 large potatoes

Half a bunch basil, shredded

2 tomatoes

1 courgette

1 aubergine

400ml extra virgin olive oil

1 lemon

1 shallot

4 baby fennel

For the tapenade:

8 olives

8 capers

1 anchovy fillet

1 teaspoon olive oil

Peel and boil the potatoes, then drain and lightly crush with a fork. Add the basil and a little olive oil, mix and season.

Skin and deseed the tomatoes, and cut into quarters. Dice the courgette and aubergine and fry in a little olive oil until cooked to a golden brown colour, adding the tomatoes for a final 30 seconds of cooking.

For the tapenade finely chop the olives, capers and anchovy and bind together with a little olive oil.

Cook the sea bass in a frying pan skin side down for three to four minutes, then turn over for a further two to three minutes. Chop the shallots and heat in a saucepan with olive oil and the juice of the lemon: season with salt and pepper.

To serve use a cutter to arrange the crushed potato in the centre of the plate; place the sea bass on top, with the vegetables around the outside. Finish the sauce with a little chopped basil then pour over the sea bass: finally, using two teaspoons shape a quenelle of tapenade to top each fillet and finish with two pieces of baby fennel.

Chocolate and crème fraîche mousse, exotic fruits and passion fruit sorbet

Serves 4

Ingredients:

450g dark chocolate

300ml whipped cream

400ml crème fraîche

4 egg yolks

150g sugar

1 each mango, paw paw, kiwi

Fresh pineapple

4 bunches of redcurrants

4 sprigs mint

Brandy snap biscuits

For the sorbet:

45 passion fruit

600ml water

400g caster sugar

1 lemon

For the syrup:

Juice and zest of 4 limes

50ml water

100g sugar

Whisk the egg yolks and sugar over a low heat to a sabayon, then leave to cool. Gently melt the chocolate and incorporate with the eggs, then add the crème fraîche and whipped cream and mix until smooth. Pour the mousse into four cylindrical plastic moulds and leave to set. Meanwhile cut the exotic fruits into a dice, and make the sorbet.

Place the mousse in the centre of the plate with a ring of diced fruit around it. Top with a brandy snap surmounted with a scoop of the sorbet: pour around a little of the lime syrup and decorate with a bunch of redcurrants and a sprig of mint.

CHEWTON GLEN

Pierre Chevillard

Salad of duck and langoustine

Serves 4

Ingredients:

8 large langoustine tails, unshelled

2 medium sized duck breasts

80g mixed leaves, washed and dried

40g celeriac chips

4 tablespoons chopped parsley

For the dressing:

10g finely chopped shallots

50ml truffle juice

5g fresh black truffles, finely chopped

100ml chicken stock

200ml olive oil

Juice of 1 lemon

Pan fry the duck breasts on the skin side very slowly until pink inside, then remove and keep warm. Pan fry the langoustine tails in a very hot pan for a few minutes: keep warm.

To make the dressing, heat the chicken stock, truffle juice and chopped truffles and reduce by half. Season to taste, add the shallots and lemon juice, then liquidize, adding the olive oil little by little until the liquid is well emulsified.

To serve toss the mixed leaves well with the dressing and arrange on the plate. Cut the duck into thin slices and arrange as a 'rosace' over the leaves; place two langoustine tails alongside. Finally sprinkle over the remaining dressing, chopped parsley, and celeriac chips.

Noisettes of lamb with a spaghetti of vegetables and garlic and thyme jus

Serves 4

Ingredients:

4 x 150g loin fillets of lamb, trimmed

120g carrots, peeled

120g leeks

120g courgettes

2 tablespoons olive oil

20g chopped parsley

For the sauce:

100g of lamb trimmings

2 cloves garlic

*40g mirepoix
(diced carrot, onion, celery)*

5g thyme

50g fresh tomatoes, diced

100ml white wine

400ml veal stock

2 tablespoons olive oil

20g butter

For the sauce, heat the olive oil in a medium sized pan and add the lamb trimmings, cooking until nicely coloured, then add the mirepoix, garlic, tomato, and thyme. Deglaze with the wine, add the veal stock and cook slowly for 50 minutes. Finally, strain the stock and reduce to coating consistency, add the butter and seasoning to taste and set aside.

Prepare the spaghetti of vegetables by slicing the carrots and leeks into thin strips, blanching for one minute in boiling water, and refreshing: the courgettes also should be sliced into 'spaghetti' strips. Heat the olive oil in a frying pan and cook the lamb loin fillets to medium rare/medium. Remove from the pan and keep warm. Add the vegetable spaghetti to the pan and sauté for three minutes, adding the parsley and seasoning to taste. Remove and keep warm.

To serve, make a neat dome for the centre of each warmed plate by twisting the spaghetti with a fork. Cut each fillet into three noisettes, and arrange around the vegetables, sprinkling over the sauce.

Summer pudding

Serves 4

Ingredients:

8 slices white bread, crusts removed

500ml raspberry purée

85g sugar

110g fresh raspberries

110g fresh strawberries

110g fresh blackcurrants

110g fresh redcurrants

Select a few berries and currants to set aside for decoration. Gently – avoid mashing – mix the rest of the fruit together with 50g of the sugar, then leave for two hours.

Cut six of the bread slices in half, and from the remaining two slices cut a small circle to fit the base of the mould and a larger disc to cover the mould when full. Soak the bread in a blend of the raspberry purée and the remaining sugar, saving a little purée for decoration.

Place a small disc at the base of each mould and line the sides with the rectangular pieces.

Fill with berries, and cover with the large discs. Seal with cling film and leave for 24 hours.

To serve turn out the mould onto a plate, pouring the remaining purée around the pudding and decorating with berries and currants.

CHILSTON PARK

Giles Stonehouse

Marinated red mullet with Provençal vegetables and a cherry tomato vinaigrette

Serves 4

This dish is best made during the summer months when all the ingredients are in plentiful supply and at their best.

The mullet:

2 x 350 – 400g red mullet, scaled, filleted and pin boned

75ml olive oil

For the marinade:

300ml virgin olive oil (the best you can afford)

75ml white wine vinegar

25ml dry white wine

To garnish:

4 cherry tomatoes

4 basil leaves

The vegetables:

50ml olive oil

50ml sunflower oil

100g aubergine, 5mm thick, dice with skin on

50g red peppers

50g green peppers

50g yellow peppers

50g red onions

100g courgettes

100g tomatoes, skinned and deseeded

1 clove garlic, chopped

Cut all vegetables into 5mm dice, ensuring that you have the correct weight once diced.

The vinaigrette:

250g vine cherry tomatoes, cut in half

2 shallots, chopped

2 sprigs of thyme

75ml olive oil

1 tablespoon plain flour

75ml red wine

1 tablespoon tomato purée

Sea salt and pepper

Red wine vinegar

Virgin olive oil (the best you can afford)

200ml water

In a heavy bottomed frying pan, heat half the oil for the vegetables and gently fry the aubergine; once soft add the onions and garlic, then remove from the pan.

Add the remaining oil and gently fry the courgettes and peppers. Once they have softened, add the aubergine mix and tomatoes; season to taste. Tip into a 2cm deep tray.

Cut each of the fish fillets into two, scoring each but taking care not to cut too deeply into the flesh. In a non-stick frying pan heat 75ml of olive oil until it is almost smoking. Season and dry the fish, then place skin side down in pan and allow the skin to crisp for 1 minute. Turn the fillets and after 30 seconds remove, placing on top of the vegetables.

Heat the ingredients for the marinade and pour over the fish fillets: cover with cling film. Allow to cool and then chill for 12 hours in the fridge.

For the vinaigrette, fry the shallots in oil, add the cherry tomatoes and allow to soften down to a compote. Add flour and thyme. Mix well and add the purée, then wine, and finally the water. Simmer for 10 minutes. Blend and strain through a fine sieve. Return to the blender and add the red wine vinegar and olive oil on medium speed. Season and allow to cool.

To present, cross-cut the skin of four firm cherry tomatoes with the stalks intact, then plunge into boiling water for 10 seconds. Remove and place in ice cold water. Peel the skin up towards the stalk, leaving it attached to the tomato.

Lightly oil 4 basil leaves and place them on a piece of kitchen paper. Microwave for 30-40 seconds until they become crisp and translucent.

Place a dessert spoon of vegetable in the centre of a chilled plate with one piece of fish on top, then another spoon of vegetables and the second piece of fish. Spoon a little marinade over the tomato stalk, pour around the tomato vinaigrette, and garnish with a cherry tomato and a basil leaf.

Roast lobster wrapped in pancetta with a haricot bean and truffle fricassée

Serves 4

Ingredients:

24 thin slices of pancetta

4 x 500g live lobsters

*300g dried haricot beans
(soaked in water overnight)*

Half a carrot, peeled

4 inches of celery stalk

2 sprigs of thyme

1 crushed clove of garlic

100ml double cream

2 shallots, chopped

*15g Truffle; cut 4 nice slices
and chop the remaining*

2 medium dried morels

*24 small courgette balls
(use a small melon scoop)*

30g unsalted butter

Bay leaf

Peppercorns

Sea salt

Prepare the haricot beans at least three hours before the meal; they can easily be prepared 24 hours in advance.

Drain the soaked beans then place them in a heavy saucepan with the celery, carrot, bay leaf, peppercorns, thyme, crushed garlic, dried morels and 2 teaspoons of sea salt. Cover with an inch of water and simmer until soft. This will take $1^1/2$ – $2^1/2$ hours depending on the size of the beans. Remove all aromatic garnish and allow to cool in the cooking liquor.

Steam the lobsters for three minutes and then remove the claws – the claws will require a further three minutes. While they are hot crack the lobster tails, using a kitchen cloth to protect your hand, and remove the tail meat intact. Wrap each tail with pancetta, roll in greaseproof paper, and then tightly wrap with foil.

Crack the claws and carefully remove all meat; repeat with the knuckles.

In a heavy saucepan fry the shallots in 30g unsalted butter until soft, then add the wine and the liquor from the beans, reducing until almost dry. Add the double cream and chopped truffle, reducing until thick, then the beans, lobster claws and knuckles, and season. Reduce the heat as the lobster will become tough if boiled. Meanwhile, place the foil packets in a hot oven for three minutes.

In large hot bowl, place a pile of the bean mix then top with lobster tail. Arrange the claws around and over the tail. Spoon over some sauce and garnish with a slice of truffle and small courgette balls that have been blanched in salted water.

Summer pudding, passion fruit jelly, and shortbread biscuit

Serves 4

For the summer pudding:

150g raspberries

150g blueberries

150g blackberries

200g strawberries (cut into quarters)

75g sugar

White bread thinly sliced

For the filling, place all the berries except the raspberries with the sugar in a pan: cover and gently heat until the sugar is dissolved and the berries are soft. Add the raspberries and remove from the heat.

Select 4 small moulds (such as a dariole mould or a small coffee cup) and line each one with cling film; wetting and wringing out the cling film will make this much easier. Remove the crusts from the thinly sliced white bread and, using a cutter, cut 8 discs of bread to the same size as the base of your mould. Now cut 4 rectangles of bread, each large enough to wrap around the inside of your mould without overlapping. Carefully dip 4 of the bread discs into the compôte, coating each side with the juices. Place the discs in the bottom of the moulds, then repeat with the sides. Drain the compôte, reserving the juices, and spoon the berries into the moulds, pressing firmly. Dip the remaining 4 discs into the reserved juices and place on top of the berries. Refrigerate overnight.

For the passion fruit jelly:

1 orange

1 pink grapefruit

3 passion fruits

4 leaves of gelatine

75g sugar

75ml water

Using a sharp knife, remove the skin and pith of the orange and grapefruit and carefully segment ensuring that each segment is pith free. Soak the gelatine leaves in cold water. In a heavy bottom pan warm the sugar and water and add the pips and juices from the passion fruits. Bring to the boil and stir in the gelatine leaves, which you have squeezed to remove any excess water. Remove from the heat and allow to cool. Arrange the segments in 4 moulds, (preferably different shaped from the Summer Puddings) and pour the cooled passion fruit over. Place in refrigerator overnight.

For the shortbread:

210g plain flour

2 small egg yolks

180g unsalted butter

90g icing sugar

Half a vanilla pod

Cream the butter and sugar in a mixing bowl, add the seeds from the vanilla pod, then the yolks and finally fold in the flour. Remove from bowl and wrap in cling film, then rest in the fridge for at least an hour.

Dust the surface and rolling pin with flour. Roll out the mix to around 5mm thick, and then cut 8 x 5cm diameter biscuits. Place on grease proof paper and bake in the oven at 150°C for 12 minutes. Remove from the oven and cool on a wire rack.

Shortbread filling:

*8 medium strawberries
(stalks removed and cut in halves)*

100ml double cream

20g icing sugar

Whip the double cream until almost peaking and add the sugar. Continue to whip until stiff. Place in a piping bag with a plain nozzle.

Take four of the cooled biscuits and pipe a twist of cream in the centre to the same height as the cut strawberries when standing. Arrange four cut strawberries around the cream, then top with the remaining biscuits and dust with icing sugar.

The sauce:

300g fresh or frozen red berries

100g icing sugar

Juice of half a lemon

Blend all the ingredients in a blender
until smooth: strain through a sieve.

4 mint leaves to garnish

To assemble the dish, carefully turn
out the summer puddings onto a tray
and coat with some of the sauce. Turn
out the passion fruit jelly, dipping the
moulds (without submerging) into
hot water until loosened. Return to
the fridge if necessary.

On a large plate place one of
each dessert, ensuring that they
don't touch. Pour some of the sauce
around the desserts and garnish with
a mint leaf.

CITY CAFE RESTAURANT, BAR & TERRACE

BRISTOL

Gary Clarke

Slow roasted aubergine and Piedmontaise pepper with fresh tortellini, red pepper dressing and pesto

Serves 4

Ingredients:

2 aubergines

2 medium red peppers

2 plum tomatoes

2 cloves garlic, peeled and thinly sliced

1 small packet fresh tortellini, preferably cheese filled

1 small pot basil pesto

100ml extra virgin olive oil

1 bunch basil (use tips for garnish)

Pinch of sea salt

For the dressing:

1 small jar sweet red pimentos

25ml balsamic vinegar

1 plum tomato

1 clove garlic, peeled and chopped

50ml pomice oil

50ml virgin olive oil

*1 bunch coriander
leaving 12 leaves for garnish*

Preheat the oven to 100°C. Halve the aubergines lengthwise and diagonally score the flesh, making sure not to cut right through; halve the red peppers and remove the seeds. Lay both out, skin sides down, on a roasting tray. Remove the stalks and halve the plum tomatoes, then insert them skin side up on the peppers. Put two or three slices of garlic on each tomato, then cover all with 50ml of the extra virgin oil and scatter moderately with sea salt. Roast for one hour, then remove and coat the aubergines while still hot with pesto and leave to cool to room temperature.

For the dressing, blend all the ingredients until smooth and strain through a fine sieve: keep at room temperature, as refrigerating will cause the dressing to separate. Adjust the oven temperature to 90°C and bring a pan of cold water with a little olive oil and salt to the boil.

Place the aubergines in the oven, at the same time immersing the tortellinin in the boiling water. While the pasta and aubergines are finishing, start preparing the presentation by laying out plates and spooning the red pepper dressing into the centre to form a circular base. Run some pesto around the rim of the dressing, take the aubergines out of the oven after five minutes and arrange on the dressing, topped with the Piedmontaise pepper. Strain the tortellini once al dente (six to eight minutes) and season with a little olive oil, salt and pepper. With a steady hand position the tortellini on the pepper, finishing with a garnish of basil tips.

Grilled halibut with cherry vine tomatoes, Kentish asparagus, spring onions and coriander dressing

Serves 4

Ingredients:

4 x 200g halibut fillets

12 cherry vine tomatoes, halved

12 spring onions, trimmed

20 medium (preferably Kentish) asparagus spears

100ml olive oil

Sea salt & freshly ground black pepper

For the dressing:

1 bunch coriander

2 tablespoons Thai fish sauce

2 cloves garlic, peeled

1 medium red chilli, deseeded and chopped

Juice of 1 lemon

Juice of 1 lime

Preheat the oven to 200°C. Place a ridged ovenproof pan over a medium temperature to heat through: it needs to be very hot when the fish goes into the oven.

Make the dressing by blending all the ingredients to form a smooth purée. Store under cover in a ceramic pot until needed.

Place a large pan of salted water on the stove to come to the boil. Season the halibut and grill with a small amount of olive oil for two minutes each side: by now the oven pan should be hot. Insert the fish and place in the oven for four to five minutes, until it is firm but not dry. Meanwhile, boil the asparagus tips for two to three minutes, strain, then add the cherry tomatoes and spring onions and keep warm.

Remove the halibut from the oven, place on a suitable tray and keep hot. Place the asparagus, cherry tomatoes and spring onions in a saucepan and lightly heat with a little olive oil. Season well, and divide onto the centre of each plate, spooning the dressing around the salad. Place the halibut on top: garnish with coriander leaves.

Vanilla crème brûlée with nut tuiles and chocolate sauce

Serves 6

Ingredients:

400ml double cream

125 milk (preferably UHT)

2 vanilla pods, split and seeds reserved

6 large free range eggs

75g caster sugar

75ml semi whipped double cream

Demerara sugar

Raspberries for garnish

Nut tuiles (makes around 24):

250g ground almonds or hazelnuts

4 large free range eggs

50g caster sugar

25g plain flour

Chocolate sauce:

100g chocolate, dark or milk

150ml double cream

Preheat the oven to 140°C. Lightly grease six ovenproof ramekins with unsalted butter and place on a baking tray.

Slowly bring the milk, semi whipped cream and vanilla pods to scalding point in a heavy based saucepan, then remove, strain, and keep hot. Beat the egg yolks in a large heatproof bowl until pale and creamy, then pour in the hot milk mix one third at a time, whisking well. Whisk in the caster sugar and vanilla seeds, and restrain into a jug. Divide the mix equally into the ramekins and bake for around 45 minutes.

Meanwhile make the tuile mix. Sift the ground nuts through a fine sieve ready for use; whisk the egg whites in a bowl until frothy but not foamy, then beat in the sugar, flour, and nuts until smooth and refrigerate until needed.

Remove the crème brûlée when the custards are slightly set on top. Test this by gently tilting one of the ramekins: the custard should come away from the edge and the centre wobble slightly. When ready, remove from the oven and leave to thicken as they cool. Chill for at least two hours before serving.

Increase the oven temperature to 180°C and lay out silicone paper on a baking sheet. Using a warmed dessert spoon, place a teaspoon of the tuile mix on the paper and spread it in a neat round using the back of the spoon. Repeat in batches of around five rounds at a time, leaving plenty of room between them. Bake until golden brown around the edges – around seven minutes – and leave on the baking sheet for a few minutes before lifting the melted sheets off with a palette knife. Drape around a rolling pin or similar to cool in the required shape. Continue in batches until there are enough tuiles.

For the chocolate sauce, break the chocolate into small pieces and place in a microwave bowl or small saucepan, depending on your preferred method. Either pour over the cream and microwave for 90 seconds on full power, or melt the chocolate in the pan over a gentle heat and stir in the cream. Leave to cool until tepid.

Decorate the plate with pools of chocolate sauce and arrange the tuiles on semi-whipped cream. Remove the crème brûlée, now completely set, from the fridge and place on a baking tray, then apply a top layer of demerara sugar to each with a teaspoon. Caramelise the sugar with a blowtorch or under a hot grill and serve with a final garnish of raspberries.

DANESFIELD HOUSE HOTEL & SPA

Damian Broom

Ballottine of eel and horseradish, Tokay gelée

Serves 4

Ingredients:

1 x 2kg eel, gutted and skinned

80g chives

50g horseradish sauce

8 litres court bouillon

Sea salt

For the gelée:

250ml Tokay

1 leaf gold gelatine

To finish:

100g Tahoon cress

1 x 25g truffle, cleaned and sliced

5g Guerandé sea salt

10ml extra virgin olive oil

Fillet the eel, season liberally with sea salt and leave to cure for twenty minutes, then pat dry. Spread the skin side with horseradish, followed by chives. Lay the eels head to tail, skin side to skin side, and wrap tightly with cling film, tying tightly with string all the way along. Wrap this tightly in muslin, also tying evenly along the whole length. Bring the court bouillon to the boil and immerse the ballottine: turn off the heat and allow the eel to cool in the liquor for three hours. Take out and refrigerate until firm.

To prepare the gelée, simply soak the gelatine in cold water, heat the wine to 70°C and dissolve the gelatine in the wine. Place the liquid in a tray to cool: when cold, refrigerate.

To serve, mix together the cress, truffle, salt and olive oil. Remove the wrappings from the eel, slice into four equal lengths and place a piece in the centre of each plate. Fork the gelée until roughly cubed, then place 3 neat piles at 12, 4, and 8 o'clock, arranging the cress mixture between them.

Blanquettes of veal belly with white truffle sauce

Serves 4

Ingredients:

1 veal belly, boned and rolled

10 litres chicken stock

1 bulb garlic

Mirepoix of vegetables

250g Alsace bacon

Bouquet garni

For the braised lentils:

300g puy lentils

4 onions

3 tablespoons 8 year old
balsamic vinegar

100ml double cream

10g chopped parsley,
tarragon, and chives

Vegetables:

100g baby asparagus

100g French beans

2 small bunches baby leeks

For the sauce:

Reduced cooking liquor

100ml double cream

1 small Alba truffle, grated

Roll the belly in muslin and tie evenly, then place in a large casserole with all the other ingredients. Bring to the boil and simmer for two and a half hours. Remove from the liquor and keep warm: pass the liquor through a fine sieve and reduce to around 250ml.

Wash the lentils and simmer until thoroughly cooked, then drain and refresh. Finely dice and sweat the onions until cooked, then deglaze with the balsamic vinegar and add the lentils. Season, add the cream, bring to the boil, and add the herbs, checking the seasoning. Blanch the vegetables in boiling salted water and refresh: when needed heat for 30 seconds in butter and water.

For the sauce, bring the reduced stock back to the boil, add the cream, and reduce by a quarter. Add the white truffle and infuse for five minutes before serving.

To serve, press the lentils firmly into a 4" ring, then place a slice of veal on top. Neatly arrange the vegetables on the veal and pour the sauce around.

Warm pear tart with Stinking Bishop ice cream

Serves 4

Ingredients:

800g all butter puff pastry
8 large pears
100g ground hazelnuts
40ml Poire William
100g caster sugar

Glacé:

2 tablespoons icing sugar,
mixed with
4 tablespoons water

Ice cream:

4 egg yolks
100g sugar
600ml cream
300ml milk
200g Stinking Bishop cheese, diced

Roll out the pastry on a floured surface to a thickness of 2mm and cut out four 100mm discs. Place the discs on a baking tray lined with silicone paper and prick liberally with a fork. Place another silicone sheet on top, then another baking tray to form a sandwich effect: this keeps the pastry flat during cooking. Cook at 200°C for eight minutes then leave to cool.

Meanwhile, peel and roughly dice four of the pears and put in a pan with the Poire William and caster sugar. Cook over a moderate heat for up to 40 minutes until it becomes a very thick dry purée, then leave to cool.

To make the ice cream, whisk the egg yolk and sugar until white. Bring the cream and milk to the boil and pour onto the egg mix, whisking continually. Transfer to a clean pan and cook out very gently until the mixture coats the back of a spoon. Whisk in the diced cheese until fully incorporated, then pass the liquid through muslin cloth. When cooled, churn in an ice cream machine until the desired consistency is reached, then put in the freezer for use.

Sprinkle the ground hazelnuts over the pre-cooked tart bases then spoon over the purée. Peel, core, and thinly slice the remaining four pears, then fan these on top of the compôte to create a rosette pattern. Brush liberally with the glacé and put in the oven at 180°C for ten minutes, applying further glacé halfway through. Place each tart in the centre of a plate with a scoop of the ice cream on top.

Michael Wignall

Assiette of smoked salmon

One side of smoked salmon will provide all the meat required for four portions

Salmon mousse:

150g smoked salmon trimmings

56g Noilly Prat

56g fish stock

1¹/₂ leaves of gelatine, soaked

280g whipping cream

10g tarragon

1 lemon, juiced

Chill the blender bowl and a mixing bowl, then blend the salmon until smooth. Boil together and reduce the Noilly Prat, fish stock and tarragon, then take off the heat and add the lemon juice and gelatine. Allow to cool.

Slowly pour the cream into the salmon in the blender bowl, keeping the mousse as cold as possible, then add the vermouth reduction a little at a time. Season to taste, pass the mousse through a fine sieve, then pipe into moulds and freeze.

Salmon rillette:

500g salmon

250g duck fat

2 tablespoons coriander, chopped

Sea salt and white pepper

Warm the duck fat, then add the salmon; remove the pan from the heat and allow to cool for five minutes, leaving the salmon in the fat. Then in a bowl finely flake the fish and mix together with three tablespoons of the confit fat, seasoning with salt and pepper. Add the coriander when cold, then press the mix into ring moulds lined with thinly sliced smoked salmon and leave to set for an hour.

Smoked salmon jelly:

4 salmon frames (carcases) with heads

2 smoked salmon skins

1$^{1}/_{2}$ bunches of tarragon

1$^{1}/_{2}$ onions with skins

Half a stick of celery

Juice of 6 limes

700ml Sauternes

10g green peppercorns

Half a leek (white only)

3.5 litres fish stock

5g saffron

4 leaves gelatine

250g smoked salmon,
cut into 25 cubes roughly 1cm x 1cm

Dice and sweat the vegetables in butter without colouring and add the lime juice. In a separate pan bring the Sauternes, saffron and peppercorns to the boil and reduce by two thirds, then add the well washed frames and skins, vegetables, chopped tarragon and fish stock and return to the boil. Simmer for 30 minutes, skimming as required, then allow to cool.

Once cool, the stock is ready for clarification. For this you will need:

5 egg whites

1 leek (white only)

1 sprig tarragon

1 small head of fennel

1 shallot, peeled

1 clove garlic

Blitz everything but the egg whites in a robot coupe for one minute, then add the whites and blitz for another 20 seconds. Pour the liquid into the cold stock and bring back to the boil, stirring constantly. When approaching boiling point, turn down the temperature and stop stirring: this will allow clarification to take place. Simmer for 25 minutes, checking for seasoning before taking off the heat.

Leave to cool for about an hour, then carefully break the surface with a ladle and gently pass the liquid through muslin into a clean bowl.

Add the gelatine leaves and pass the liquid a second time, then line a tray 15 x 30 x 2.5cm deep with cling film and pour in the jelly mix to a depth of about half a centimetre.

Keep the jelly liquid warm while the base layer sets in the fridge, then arrange the cubes of salmon at regular intervals over the tray. Pour warm jelly mix around and over the cubes, then allow this second layer to set. Finally pour in the remaining jelly and leave to set for at least two hours before cutting out the jellies for serving. This should always be done with a warm thin knife at the last possible moment: trim the cubes for an even appearance.

Ballotine of smoked salmon on tomato fondue:

10 Roma plum tomatoes,
skinned, deseeded and diced

50ml olive oil

1 sprig thyme

4 anchovy fillets, diced

Half a clove of garlic, diced

10 black olives, stoned and diced

Using only the thick part of a side of salmon, cut out strips 2cm x 2cm x 25cm: you should get four strips from the side. Roll each strip very tightly in cling film to form a cylinder, then tie the ends of each cylinder tightly with string and leave for twelve hours.

When ready to serve, cut to the desired size leaving the cling film on to hold the shape. Seal both ends to a light golden brown, then carefully remove the cling film and brush with olive oil immediately prior to serving on the fondue.

To prepare the fondue, place all the ingredients in a heavy saucepan and cook slowly for around thirty minutes until all the oil is absorbed and the liquid has evaporated. Place a small quantity of the fondue on each plate, with the seared and oiled ballotine on top.

Smoked salmon terrine:

150g foie gras, sliced

250g smoked salmon

3 large potatoes

2 x 250g clarified butter

100g girolles

200g smoked salmon rillette

Peel and cut the potatoes into strips of about 10 x 5cm and 2mm thick. Heat the butter in a wide frying pan and very slowly heat the potato until it is just cooked: without colour but pliable. Remove the strips from the pan and place on a tray to cool. When cool, line the terrine mould with the potato, ensuring that the strips butt but do not overlap. Place the lined mould in the fridge to stay cool.

Gently fry the sliced foie gras in butter for one minute each side, then remove and cool. Fry the girolles for one minute, seasoning to taste, and cut the salmon into strips 30 x 4cm wide and around 5mm thick.

To assemble the terrine, apply a thin layer (around 2.5mm) of the rillette at the bottom of the potato lined mould. Allow this layer to set, then add the rest of the ingredients in further layers as follows, allowing each layer to set in position before adding the next: foie gras, smoked salmon, rillette, girolles, smoked salmon, rillette. Finally, apply sufficient pressure to make the terrine firm enough to turn over. Leave to set overnight.

Frogs legs with a ravioli of oxtail

Serves 4

Ingredients:

300g frogs legs, trimmed and jointed

20 tomato petals, confit

2 heads chicory

20g trompette mushrooms

20g girolles

4 beetroots, raw

1 oxtail, trimmed and jointed

10g truffle

10 Thai asparagus

For the pasta:

510g pasta flour

10ml olive oil

4 whole eggs

5 egg yolks

2 tablespoons Pommery mustard

For the pea velouté:

200g frozen peas

200g chicken stock

For the marinade:

1 litre red wine
(also required for the beetroot)

1 clove garlic

1 bay leaf

1 teaspoon fresh mixed herbs

1 teaspoon chopped parsley

1 teaspoon chopped thyme

For the fondant beetroot:

200ml water

50ml red wine vinegar

25g caster sugar

Place the oxtail in a pan, cover with wine, chopped garlic and the bay leaf, and leave to marinate overnight. Remove and dry the oxtail, then seal it in a very hot pan until golden brown all over. Place in a saucepan and cover with wine and herbs, then slowly bring to the boil, skimming constantly, and simmer for two to three hours until tender. Take the oxtail out of the cooking liquor and pick the meat off the bone and into a bowl: reduce the liquid by two thirds and pour a small amount over the meat. Season to taste. Add the thyme and parsley and shape the mix into four golf ball sized spheres, then lightly fry each ball, squeeze dry in a cloth, and place in the fridge to cool.

To prepare the pasta, put the flour in a robot coupe and whisk together the other ingredients in a bowl with a pinch of salt. Add the mix to the blender; after a minute, stop the machine and divide the mix into three. Process for a further minute, take out and knead the dough for one minute, then leave to rest for two hours. Once the dough has rested, roll out to '0' setting on the pasta machine and cut into eight discs 10cm in diameter. Egg wash one disc lightly and place an oxtail ball in the centre, then seal a second disc on top: it is vital that this is done without air bubbles or cracks. Trim the seal, then repeat the process for the other ravioli, place on butter paper and refrigerate until needed.

Make a pea velouté by blitzing the frozen peas in a liquidizer, pouring in the chicken stock during processing. Continue until a smooth paste is achieved, then pass, seasoning to taste. To prepare the fondant beetroot, slice each of the four beetroot into three, at around 2cm thickness, then using a 4cm circular cutter create into discs of equal size. In a deep pan, cover the discs with 200ml red wine, the water, red wine vinegar, and caster sugar. Simmer for about 30 minutes, checking after twenty to see whether cooked: then extract the beetroot and reduce the liquid by two thirds to create a glazing syrup.

To serve, sauté the frogs legs in a little olive oil for one to two minutes, depending on size. Reheat the beetroot in the syrup and blanch the other vegetables in salted boiling water: wilt the chicory in a small amount of water, butter and salt until tender, and immerse the ravioli in simmering salted water for four and a half minutes. Slowly heat, but do not boil, the velouté. Arrange the fondant beetroot in the centre of a bowl, with the vegetables around the rim: take the ravioli out of the water, season, and place on the beetroot: finally, foam the pea velouté with a hand blender and spoon over the ravioli.

Apple mousse

Serves 4

Ingredients:

5 egg whites

200g caster sugar

100g water

30g icing sugar

4 egg yolks

4 leaves gelatine

200g unsalted butter, diced

260g double cream

1 teaspoon cornflour

5 Bramley apples, peeled and chopped

100g cold water

Bring the apples and water to the boil, simmer for five minutes, then blend, pass, and allow to cool. Reheat gently in a pan with the cornflour, slowly adding the diced butter; remove from the heat and allow to cool for two minutes, then blend in the egg yolks and dissolve the gelatine.

Heat the caster sugar and water to soft ball in a pan. Meanwhile, whisk the egg whites to soft peak in a mixer; slowly add the icing sugar, then the hot syrup, and continue whisking until cold.

Fold the meringue into the purée mix, then semi-whip and add the cream, pour the mixture into moulds and leave to set. Warm the moulds for a few seconds before serving to release the mousse, then turn out onto plates.

Apple skin sorbet:

400g Granny Smith apple skins (frozen)

Juice of 1 1/2 lemons

380g sorbet syrup

Blitz the skins with the syrup, pass and churn. The sorbet needs to be kept very cold to preserve the vivid green colour.

For the Anglaise:

4 egg yolks

500ml semi-skimmed milk

75g caster sugar

2 vanilla pods

Whisk the yolks and sugar together until white and doubled in size (sabayon). Slice the vanilla pods in two and bring them to boil in the milk, then pour over the sabayon. In a clean pan, return the mix to the heat and slowly cook for five minutes, then pass. The result will be a very thin Anglaise, which will hold for longer when foamed.

Apple springs:

5 Granny Smith apples, peeled

2 litres water

325g sugar

Juice of 2 lemons

Bring the ingredients for the soaking syrup to the boil and simmer for five minutes. With a potato peeler, peel the apples on a chopping board into strips roughly 1 cm wide by 30cm long. Repeat until you have ten strips, then place the strips in the soaking syrup overnight.

Extract the strips from the syrup, and place on a baking mat in the oven at 90°C for two and a half hours or until dry, then turn the oven up to 120° and bake for a further 3 minutes. Take out the strips and wind them (like tuiles) around a cylinder approximately 2cm in diameter. To preserve, the springs must be kept with silica gel in an airtight container.

Assemble the dish as shown.

ESSEBORNE MANOR HOTEL

David Morris

Rosettes of seasonal melon with mango, prosciutto, and chilli salsa

Serves 4

Ingredients:

4 medium gala melons

4 sprigs chervil

For the salsa:

1 firm mango

1 small red onion

1 red chilli

3 slices prosciutto

1 tablespoon finely chopped parsley

Sea salt

Extra virgin olive oil

Top and tail the melons, cut each in half across the middle, peel, and remove the seeds. On a meat slicer, cut into slices approximately 1.5mm thick, using the whole melon, then place the slices in the fridge while making the salsa.

Peel the mango and remove the flesh from the stone, then very finely dice the flesh and place in a bowl. Prepare the other ingredients to the same fine dice (brunoise), season with a little sea salt and drizzle on oil until the mix is loose.

To build the rosettes, fold each slice of melon in half, place in the hand and roll from one end to the other to form a conical rosette. Place the first cone in the middle of the plate: from here other rosettes can be added to make a circular base layer. Place further layers on top, continuing the process using up to 21 rosettes: the result should be a natural dome. To enhance the shape place a sheet of cling film over the dome and cup with the hands (the film can be left in place until serving).

Spoon salsa around the base of the melon, and arrange the chervil at intervals around each dome.

Duo of rabbit with root vegetables, cocotte potatoes and port sauce

Serves 4

Ingredients:

2 rabbits

1 chicken breast

40 slices pancetta

Fenugreek

Rosemary

Bay leaf

2 red onions

60g girolles

Crepinette

16 new potatoes

Root vegetables, eg:

Carrot

Kohlrabi

Shallots

Swede

Beetroot

Potatoes

For the sauce:

40ml port

1 litre reduced veal stock

60g mushrooms

2 shallots

Rosemary

Thyme

Remove the legs from the rabbit and take out the thigh bones. Take the loins off the back and trim off any excess fat and sinew (if your butcher is preparing the meat, be sure to keep all the leftovers). Place the bones and carcass in a pan with the trimmings from the vegetable prep, cover with water, and bring to the boil. Leave to simmer for around 40 minutes, then reduce by 80%.

Prepare the farce: mince the chicken breast and sauté with the chopped red onions and chopped girolles; season, then drain. When cold add the chopped fenugreek and again check the seasoning.

Lay out the crepinette in four 6" squares; place a bay leaf in the middle of each then lay out 5 slices of pancetta topped with a rabbit leg. Roll up the whole, sealing with cling film to make a tight cylinder, then poach in the reduced rabbit stock for 45 minutes. Repeat the process for the loins, but with the addition of a piped tube of the farce alongside the meat. The loin cylinders require no more than ten minutes poaching time, so add to the stock when the legs have been in for 35 minutes. On completion, remove the cling film and pat dry.

Meanwhile, turn the root vegetables and blanch each individually as they will require different cooking times. Prepare the sliced beetroot separately by tossing it in butter.

Place 100g of butter together with the rosemary and all the vegetables except the beetroot in a pan lined with foil: this goes into a hot oven (180°C) for around 20 minutes.

For the cocotte potatoes, turn until about the size of your thumb. Blanche until almost cooked, then finish in butter and a little reduced veal stock.

For the sauce, chop the shallots, slice the button mushrooms, and place in a saucepan; add the port and bring to the boil. Add the reduced rabbit stock and reduce by half, then add the reduced veal stock and herbs, simmer, and pass through a muslin.

Before serving, place the leg and loin portions in a hot sauté pan with a little butter and gently add colour. Remove the veg from the oven. To plate, slice a little from the leg to provide a base for standing, then slice the loins diagonally and position alongside the leg. Arrange the veg around the plate with the beetroot and potatoes; finish with the sauce.

Hot chocolate fondant with pistachio ice cream

Serves 5

For the fondant:

125g dark chocolate

125g unsalted butter

60g caster sugar

25g plain flour

3 egg yolks

2 whole eggs

Butter and sugar the inside of five dariole moulds. Very gently melt the butter and chocolate over a bain marie; cream the eggs, yolks, and sugar, and fold into the melted mixture. Finally, carefully add the flour, ensuring that it has fully combined, then place in the moulds and cook for twelve minutes at 200°C.

For the pistachio ice cream, mix 750g of crème Anglaise and a quarter of a teaspoon of pistachio paste in an ice cream machine one day in advance and freeze.

For a tuile, melt 100g of butter and add 100g of Fang sugar, 100g of plain flour, and 2 egg whites: blend together, allow to cool, and chill.

FAIRYHILL

Paul Davies

Scrambled eggs with cockles and roasted peppers

Serves 4

Ingredients:

1 red and 1 yellow pepper, roasted and cut in strips (see below)

Olive oil

4 slices bread

2 cloves garlic, halved

8 eggs

150ml double cream

100g fresh cockles

Chopped chives

Place the peppers in an oven at 180°C until they are brown and blistered, then remove and put in a plastic bag to cool. When cool split each pepper in half, removing the seeds and skin. Cut into 5mm strips and put to one side.

Cut 3 heart shaped croûtons from each slice of bread. Rub both sides with cut garlic, then fry in olive oil until golden and crisp. Drain well and put aside to keep warm.

Whisk the eggs and cream together with some black pepper. Place a little olive oil in a pan and add most of the peppers (reserve 4 red and 4 yellow strips for garnish). Add the egg mixture and start to scramble; when half scrambled, add the cockles and continue to cook until the desired consistency is achieved.

To serve, place three croûtons on each plate and arrange the scrambled eggs in the middle with a cross of pepper on top of each portion. Finish by sprinkling with chopped chives.

Loin of venison with apple and fresh coriander

Serves 4

Ingredients:

A half loin of venison

Venison bones

2 large cooking apples

2 eating apples

1 bunch fresh coriander

Dried coriander

1 onion

Breadcrumbs

Lemon juice

330ml cider

To make a rich stock, first roast the bones, then place them in a pan with two litres of water and some roughly chopped carrots, leeks and celery, together with a bouquet garni. Bring to the boil and simmer for an hour, then reduce to around 500ml.

Trim the venison so that only the eye of the meat remains. Divide the trimmed meat into steaks, then put to one side. Finely mince trimmings together with the onion, breadcrumbs and the stalks of the fresh coriander. Add seasoning, then either pass through a sausage-making machine or form into a sausage shape by hand.

Peel the cooking apples and immerse immediately in water to which lemon juice and salt has been added, keeping the apple as white as possible. Drain, then cook with 50ml of the cider to make a smooth apple purée. Meanwhile, cut the eating apples into wedges and immerse in lemon juice and water.

Check the seasoning of the stock, then add the rest of the cider and reduce again to around 250ml. Pre-heat a griddle or heavy-based frying pan and cook the sausage until browned all over. Dip each venison steak in ground coriander and cook to the desired degree. At the same time griddle the apple slices, warm through the apple purée, adding the chopped fresh coriander leaves.

To assemble the dish, place the purée in the middle of the plate: slice the venison and arrange in a fan, with the sausage sliced in two. Garnish with the apple slices and surround with the jus.

Roast peach with lemon crème caramel

Serves 4

Ingredients:

4 Peaches

275ml Stock syrup

For the lemon custard:

275ml milk

1 whole free-range egg

2 free-range egg yolks

125g caster sugar

1 lemon (zest and juice)

Half a vanilla pod

For the shortbread biscuits:

250g soft butter

50g rice flour

75g icing sugar

350g plain flour

For the caramel:

200g caster sugar

100ml water

Bring the stock syrup to the boil and lightly poach the peaches: allow them to cool, then peel.

Place the sugar into a heavy-bottomed saucepan with 75ml of water. Bring to the caramel stage, then remove from the heat and add the rest of the cold water to prevent the caramel from burning. Pour the caramel into moulds.

For the custard, split the vanilla pod, put it, seeds included, in a pan with the milk and bring to the boil. Meanwhile, whisk the sugar, lemon zest and juice together with the eggs until all the sugar is dissolved. Pour the hot milk onto the lemon mixture while stirring constantly, then place the custard back on to a low heat and stir until the mixture begins to thicken. Carefully pour into caramel moulds and cook in a bain marie in the oven at 170˚C for 30-40 minutes.

To prepare the shortbread biscuits, mix all the ingredients in a large bowl until a dough is formed. Roll out to the thickness required and cut to shape. Cook at 180˚C for 10-15 minutes. Allow to cool, then dust with caster sugar.

Kevin Mangeolles

Roast breast of grouse with sweetcorn purée

Serves 4

2 grouse

For the foie gras & grouse parfait:
Legs from the two grouse
40g foie gras
1 egg
50g chicken stock
75g cream
$1/4$ zest orange
$1/2$ teaspoon salt

For the purée:
2 sweetcorn
100g butter
Nutmeg and salt to season

For the sherry jelly:
100g veal (or chicken) stock
150g sherry
1 leaf gelatine

Boil the sweetcorn for one and a half hours, then scrape off the corn and mix to a smooth paste in a blender. Season with salt and nutmeg, then pass through a fine sieve and set the purée to one side.

For the parfait, blend all the ingredients to a smooth paste and pass, then place the mixture in butter moulds and cook for eight minutes in a water bath at 100°C.

To make the jelly, boil together the sherry and stock while soaking the gelatine. Season with salt, add the gelatine, and leave to set in the fridge in a square tray. Cut into squares to serve.

To cook the grouse, seal the breasts on the bone, two at a time in 25g of butter per bird. Roast for eight to ten minutes at 170°C, then rest for ten minutes. Carve the meat off the bone before serving.

Braised veal with sweetbread, carrot purée and a pollen crust

Serves 6

Ingredients:

1kg veal belly

450g sweetbreads

75g carrots, chopped

75g leeks, chopped

75g onions

6 tomatoes, chopped

Half a head of garlic

1 litre veal (or chicken) stock

375ml white wine

25g chives, chopped

For the purée:

500g carrots

400g chicken stock

200g butter

For the crust:

10g shallots, chopped

50g butter

75g breadcrumbs

10g pollen

To garnish:

Baby carrots

Bacon crisps

Spinach

Sweat all the vegetables in a roasting tray, then add the chopped tomatoes, white wine and veal stock. Add the veal and braise for six hours at 130°C. When the meat is cooked remove it from the stock and cut into rectangles: continue reducing the cooking liquor until it thickens, then add the chives.

Blanch the sweetbreads in boiling water, then cut into equal portions and roast in hot oil and butter for ten minutes at 150°C. Blend the ingredients for the pollen crust together, then sprinkle the pollen crust over the sweetbreads as soon as they come out of the oven. Leave to rest for ten minutes.

To prepare the purée, boil the carrots in the chicken stock and when soft liquidise, adding the chopped butter. Pass through a fine strainer and season with salt.

Carpaccio of pineapple with nougat glace

Serves 4

4 Baby pineapple sliced very thinly

Pistachio jelly:

25g white wine

12g pistachio purée

80g stock syrup

1 leaf bronze gelatine

Biscotti:

75g pistachio

100g flour

1 whole egg

1 egg yolk

10g melted butter

1/4 teaspoon mixed spice

75g sugar

Nougat:

75g egg whites

50g honey

80g sugar

40g water

500g whipped cream

50g sugar

20g pistachios

20g hazelnuts

20g cherries

To prepare the jelly, boil together the wine, purée, and syrup, then dissolve the gelatine in the liquid and leave to set in the fridge.

For the biscotti, mix together all the ingredients: when fully integrated, roll out on a baking tray to a thickness of around 1cm. Slice very thinly and bake at 170°C for five minutes.

Make an Italian meringue by boiling together the 80g of sugar, water and honey to 110°C. Meanwhile whisk the egg whites; when they have doubled in volume pour in the hot syrup, fold in the cream, and whisk until cold.

Boil the 50g of sugar on its own to caramel, then add and coat the nuts. Pour out the mix onto a baking sheet and leave to set, then chop the cherries, break the nut caramel unto small chunks, and mix both into the meringue. Pour the blend into moulds and freeze ready for serving.

Caramelise 12 of the pineapple slices, using the rest as the base of the assembly. Serve as shown.

THE GIBBON BRIDGE HOTEL

Head Chef: **Gary Buxton**
Proprietor: **Janet Simpson**

Risotto dumplings of smoked trout and smoked haddock

Serves 4 to 6

Ingredients:

1 red onion, peeled and diced

2 cloves of garlic, crushed

2 tablespoons of olive oil

350g Arborio rice

1 smoked trout

1 fillet of smoked haddock

1$^1/_2$ litres chicken stock

50g Parmesan

2 tablespoons chopped parsley

Flour, beaten egg and dry breadcrumbs for coating

Oil for frying

Juice of 1 lemon

Sauté the onion and garlic in olive oil and butter over a low heat until soft: add the rice and stir until coated, then add 250ml of stock and stir again. Allow the stock to absorb before adding another 250ml. Continue adding stock, stirring frequently until the rice is cooked, then add the flaked trout, haddock, Parmesan, lemon juice, and parsley. Season to taste, pour into a dish and allow to cool. Finally divide the risotto into golf ball size rounds and pass these through the coating mixture of flour, egg and breadcrumbs.

Green bean & red onion salsa:

$^1/_2$ cup chopped fine beans

1 bunch flat leaf parsley

$^1/_2$ bunch chives, cut into batons

Juice of 2 lemons

1$^1/_2$ red onions, finely chopped

2 tablespoons olive oil

Mix all the above together, then put in the fridge for use when required.

Horseradish & grain mustard mayonnaise:

250ml mayonnaise

2 tablespoons horseradish

$^1/_2$ tablespoon grain mustard

$^1/_2$ teaspoon chopped chervil

Mix all the ingredients together and season to taste.

To assemble, deep fry the dumplings for three to four minutes at 170ºc, remove from the fryer and leave to drain; meanwhile, place a little horseradish mayonnaise in the centre of a plate. Now place 3 of the balls onto the mayonnaise, with the salsa on top of the balls. For extra garnish, drizzle a little olive oil and balsamic vinegar around the outside of the plate and finish with a few Parmesan shavings.

Fillet of beef with bubble & squeak, broad beans and shallots

Serves 4

Ingredients:

*4 x 225g fillet steaks
trimmed of any sinew or fat*

2 large Maris Piper potatoes

1 spring cabbage

1 pinch nutmeg

1 egg yolk

*40 broad beans,
blanched and removed from skin*

*20 small shallots,
peeled and blanched for 4 minutes*

300ml beef stock

200ml Madeira

A little oil

A pinch of sugar & flour

Wash the potatoes, peel and chop into one inch dice, then cover with salted water in a saucepan and bring to the boil. Simmer for 15 to 20 minutes; when cooked drain and dry out on the top of the stove for one minute, then mash.

Next prepare the cabbage by shredding the inner and outer leaves (keeping them separate) as finely as possible. Blanch the inner leaves in boiling salted water for one to two minutes: remove and leave to cool, then combine with the potato, nutmeg and egg yolk. Shape into 2" cakes, using a little flour to prevent the mash sticking to your hands. Finally, make the sauce by reducing the Madeira by a third and then adding the beef stock: simmer until the sauce coats the back of a spoon.

Place a large frying pan on a high heat. Season the steaks well, drizzle a little oil into the pan and add the steaks. When they are sealed on one side turn them over, add the butter and shallots, and continue cooking to your preference. Meanwhile deep fry the outer shredded leaves of the cabbage for 20 to 30 seconds or until crisp and sprinkle with a little sugar and salt.

To assemble, shallow fry the bubble and squeak cakes until they are golden on each side, place a steak on top of a cake in the centre of each plate, and arrange the shallots around the steak. Add the broad beans to the sauce and trace over and around the steak: top with the deep fried cabbage and serve.

Strawberries and cream layered with praline wafers

Serves 4

Ingredients:

750g caster sugar

75g sliced almonds

450ml double cream

2-3 drops vanilla essence

500g strawberries

150ml strawberry coulis

150ml yoghurt

2 sheets silicone paper

50g icing sugar

Place the caster sugar and enough water to just cover it in a high sided pan over a high heat; bring to the boil and simmer until a light caramel colour is achieved. Pour the liquid onto a sheet of silicone paper, sprinkle the almonds over the top, and allow to cool.

Next break the now hard praline into smaller pieces and place in a blender, blitzing until it is the texture of breadcrumbs. Spread another sheet of silicone paper onto a baking tray and spoon the crumbed praline onto the paper, spreading it into 4" discs. Place in the oven until the crumbs melt down (between two and four minutes) then remove and allow to cool once again.

Whip the cream with a little icing sugar and vanilla essence and wash and prepare the strawberries by removing the top and cutting each in half.

To assemble, place a praline disc in the centre of each plate, pipe a little of the cream on top then arrange the strawberries on top of the cream: repeat this once more and finish with a disc on top. Finally pour the strawberry coulis around the discs, garnish with a little yoghurt and dust with icing sugar.

CITY CAFE RESTAURANT, BAR & TERRACE

GLASGOW

Richard Lyth

Rabbit and walnut salad with orange dressing

Serves 4

Ingredients:

4 fillets of rabbit

4 rabbit kidneys (optional)

4 oranges, segmented

12 walnuts

Salad leaves;
eg frisée, rocket, mâche, radish sprouts

Pickled chervil

50g butter

Vinaigrette

For the orange dressing:

200ml orange juice

200ml light olive oil

1 teaspoon Dijon mustard

1 egg yolk

1 pinch Cayenne pepper

To make the dressing, simply blitz all the ingredients together with a hand blender to the consistency of a liquid mayonnaise.

Sauté the fillets – and the kidneys if being used – in the butter for three to four minutes, then take out and set aside to keep warm. Toss the leaves in a little vinaigrette, then place the salad in the centre of the plate: carve the rabbit and arrange the slices on top, then garnish with the orange segments, walnuts, and pickled chervil. Drizzle the orange dressing over the dish to finish.

Roasted cod and braised beef

Serves 4

Turbot or halibut are excellent substitutes for this dish

Ingredients:

4 x 180g cod fillets

50g olive oil

50g butter

1kg beef skirt or oxtail

200g onion, sliced

300ml claret

1 large sprig thyme

2 carrots, chopped

3 bay leaves

1 head of garlic, split

Sunflower oil

500ml chicken stock

For the vegetables:

100ml double cream

100ml red wine

100ml chicken stock

100g butter

1 Savoy cabbage, heart only

20 shallots

20-30 cèpes or button mushrooms

Seal the meat in the oil on a hot pan, then season and place in a casserole; fry off the onions, garlic and carrots until lightly caramelised then add to the pot. Add the wine and herbs, bring to the boil, and reduce the liquid by half. Meanwhile, bring the chicken stock to the boil and add to the reduction. Lower the heat to a simmer, adding water if there is not enough liquid to cover the meat, then cover with a lid and cook in the oven for up to three hours at 150°C until the meat is tender. Remove the meat from the pot and keep warm. Strain the liquid and bring it back to the boil in a clean pan, skimming off the fat, and reduce to a good thick sauce consistency. Finally, return the meat to the pan and keep warm.

To prepare the vegetables, sear the shallots in a little hot oil then deglaze the pan with the red wine and chicken stock. Simmer until the shallots are cooked and season slightly. The mushrooms are sautéed in the butter until coloured, then seasoned. Finely slice the inner leaves of the cabbage, blanch and refresh, then reheat with the cream to bind.

Sear the fish in the butter and olive oil and roast in the oven at 180°C until cooked through, around four to five minutes. Dress the cabbage on the plate and top with braised meat: surround with shallots and mushrooms. Place the fish on top and spoon extra meat sauce around the dish.

White chocolate and raspberry mousse

Serves 4

Ingredients:

200ml full cream milk

1 vanilla pod

2 sheets gelatine

250g good quality white chocolate

250g whipping cream

250g fresh raspberries

Infuse the milk with the vanilla over a low heat; soften the gelatine in cold water for four minutes; chop the chocolate and put it in a stainless steel bowl. Pour half the milk over the chocolate and whisk to melt the chocolate. Drain the gelatine well and add it to the rest of the milk; once it has fully dissolved add the liquid to the chocolate , mix well, and leave to cool.

Cover the base of four moulds with raspberries. Fold the cream, lightly whipped, into the cooled chocolate and pour the mousse into the moulds. Level the top surfaces and place in the fridge to set for six to eight hours. When ready to serve, turn out the moulds and decorate the plate with raspberry coulis and chocolate shavings.

Brett Sutton

Pressed tomato timbale, goats cheese and basil fondant and 25 year old balsamic vinegar

Serves 4

For the timbale:

16 plum tomatoes

8 vine tomatoes

64 tarragon leaves

For the fondant:

250g goat's cheese

1 clove garlic

2 tablespoons basil, finely shredded

To garnish:

24 red chard leaves

2 banana shallots

4 bread stick croûtes

25 year old balsamic vinegar

Olive oil

4 sprigs chervil

To make the tomato timbales, line four dariole moulds with cling film. Blanch, refresh, de-skin and de-seed the plum tomatoes, then dry the flesh on some kitchen towel. Meanwhile, roast the vine tomatoes for eight minutes at 180°C, then blend to a smooth purée in a blender.

Next place two cheeks of plum tomato into the bottom of each ring mould, season well, and cover with two leaves of tarragon and a teaspoon of the puréed vine tomatoes; repeat to the top of the mould. Wrap in cling film, and refrigerate for at least 8 hours with a small weight pressing each timbale.

To make the goat's cheese fondant, purée the goats cheese with the garlic and 50ml of water. Spoon the finely shredded basil into the mix, season well, and refrigerate.

Prepare shallot rings by finely slicing the shallots across their width. Turn out the tomato cakes from the moulds and place on top of a small dressed salad of red chard. Top each tomato cake with a bread stick croûte, with a quenelle of the goats cheese fondant on top of the croûte; drizzle around the olive oil and the 25 yr old balsamic vinegar, and garnish with chervil.

Roasted scallops and John Dory with langoustines, truffle pomme purée, black and white puddings and Madeira sauce

Serves 4

Ingredients:

12 diver caught scallops

8 fillets John Dory

12 langoustines

For the pomme purée:

4 large potatoes

3-5 tablespoons truffle oil (to taste)

For the Madeira sauce:

375ml red wine

1.25 litres chicken stock

700ml veal stock

375ml Madeira

To garnish:

12 slices black pudding

12 slices white pudding

12 sprigs chervil

25 year old balsamic vinegar

Olive oil

Prepare and clean the scallops well, discarding the coral: prepare the John Dory and langoustines.

For the pomme purée season the boiled and drained potatoes, then blend to a purée either by hand or in a moulis, adding the truffle oil to taste.

Make the Madeira sauce by reducing red wine to a quarter, add the chicken stock and reduce to a quarter again, add the Madeira and reduce by a half, then add the veal stock, season, and sieve.

To serve, pan fry the John Dory and the scallops in oil and butter for two minutes each side; steam the langoustines for about a minute. Pan fry the black and white puddings, reheat the pomme purée and the sauce, and arrange on the plate as shown above.

Assiette of red berry British desserts

Serves 4

For the Eton mess:

100ml whipping cream

50g sieved icing sugar

75g English strawberries

100g dried meringue

To make the Eton mess whisk the whipping cream with the sugar to stiff peaks. Cut the strawberries into quarters and add to the cream mix, then finally fold in the dried meringue and spoon into moulds.

For the Summer pudding:

*1 punnet each:
  strawberries,
  raspberries,
  redcurrants*

200ml stock syrup

8 slices white bread

To make the summer puddings, purée the fruit – keeping back a few of each of the berries – with the stock syrup and pass the liquid through a chinois.

Using a dariole mould cut discs of white bread to cover the base and top of the moulds, with rectangular strips for the sides. Line the moulds with cling film, leaving sufficient overhang to allow a good seal when the mould is full. Soak the bread pieces in the fruit purée, then put the bases and sides into position in the moulds.

Chop the remaining strawberries, raspberries and redcurrants and mix them into the fruit purée, then spoon the mix into the dariole mould: slightly overfill the mould as the filling will contract as it sets.

Finally place the bread 'lid' onto the mould and seal the top with the cling film. Press in the fridge under a light weight for 24 hours.

For the baked Alaska:

8 whole eggs

250g sugar

250g flour

500ml vanilla ice cream

8 strawberries, sliced lengthwise

Framboise liqueur

Meringue:

4 egg whites

100g caster sugar

Make a sheet of génoise sponge by whisking the eggs with the sugar until light, fluffy and pale, then fold in the flour. Bake on a greased sheet for 10-15 minutes at 180°C: use a knife to check that the sponge is fully baked. Cut out four rings and drizzle with framboise to soak into the sponge. Place a scoop of vanilla ice cream in the middle of each disc, slightly smaller than the diameter of the sponge to allow slices of strawberries to be placed around the ice cream.

Next prepare the meringue. Whisk the egg whites with a pinch of salt to stiff peaks, then add the caster sugar and continue whisking until firm. Spoon this onto the sponge and ice-cream base, ensuring it is totally covered, then cook in a hot oven for four mins. Serve straight from the oven.

Shown here with the summer pudding served with a ball of basil and lemon sorbet in a sugar cage and the Eton mess decorated with a strawberry tuile.

LODGE & SPA AT INCHYDONEY ISLAND
Mark Kirby

Tian of cured salmon & crab with red pepper and wasabi crème fraîche

Serves 8

Ingredients:

450g salmon fillet

250g white crab meat

1 tablespoon lumpfish roe

2 tablespoons chopped coriander

Zest of half a lemon

1 teaspoon crème fraîche

1 tablespoon salt

1 tablespoon caster sugar

$^{1}/_{2}$ teaspoon Dijon mustard

4 tablespoons crème fraîche to garnish

1 cucumber, finely sliced

Lemon juice to taste

For the sauce:

1 medium red pepper

2 tablespoons crème fraîche

$^{1}/_{2}$ teaspoon wasabi

1 teaspoon lemon juice

Remove the skin from the salmon and extract any bones with tweezers. Mix the tablespoon of salt and the sugar in a bowl with the lemon zest and rub the mixture into both sides of the fish; seal well in cling film and refrigerate for twelve hours. Rinse the marinated salmon well under cold running water and dry with a clean cloth, then cut into half inch cubes and mix with the crab meat, mustard, coriander, lemon juice and crème fraîche. Season with salt and pepper.

To prepare the sauce, place the peppers into a hot oven until the skins blacken, then remove. When cool, remove the skins and seeds and place in a blender with the other sauce ingredients, blending until smooth.

To serve, place a pastry cutter in the centre of the plate and fill with the salmon and crab, gently pressing down with the back of a spoon to leave about a tenth of the ring empty. Top with crème fraîche, and smooth the surface with a spatula, then garnish with lumpfish roe. Finally, position cucumber slices around the central arrangement and decorate with the sauce.

Seared fillet of (local) sea bass with stir fried vegetables and coriander

Serves 4

Ingredients:

*4 medium sized sea bass fillets,
scales removed and filleted*

2 tablespoons lemon juice

3 tablespoons light soy sauce

*$1/2$ teaspoon red chilli,
deseeded and chopped*

1 tablespoon vegetable oil

150g leek cut into thin strips

50g oyster mushrooms

*1 red pepper,
deseeded and cut into strips*

8 heads baby corn, halved lengthways

50ml fish stock

1 tablespoon fresh coriander, chopped

1 clove garlic, chopped

*Piece of fresh root ginger,
peeled and grated*

*Sea salt
& freshly ground black pepper*

Make three diagonal cuts around 3" long on the skin side of each sea bass fillet. Mix one tablespoon each of the lemon juice and soy sauce and sprinkle over the fillets: add salt and pepper.

Steam the sea bass for around eight minutes (depending on the thickness of the fillets). Meanwhile, heat the oil in a non stick pan and add the garlic, ginger, leek, pepper, baby corn and mushrooms and gently sauté for one minute. Add the fish stock and the remaining lemon juice and soy sauce: simmer for a further two to three minutes, adding the coriander at the last minute. To serve, place the fish on the crispy vegetables.

Mixed summer berries with a warm red wine and orange juice flavoured with cinnamon

Serves 8

Ingredients:

30ml red wine

200ml fresh orange juice

4 teaspoons Grand Marnier

4 teaspoons cornflour

120g light Muscovado sugar

8 sticks of cinnamon

400g strawberries, halved

200g raspberries

200g blueberries

Dissolve the cornflour in the Grand Marnier and 50ml of the orange juice. In a saucepan bring the remainder of the orange juice, the red wine, sugar, and cinnamon sticks to the boil: add the dissolved cornflour and simmer for two minutes. Pass the liquid through a sieve and keep warm.

Arrange the prepared berries in serving bowls and pour over the warm sauce: serve either on its own or with a sorbet.

KINNAIRD

Trevor Brooks

Foie gras terrine with Wigmore cheese and caramelised apple

16 portions

Ingredients:

1 whole duck foie gras

300g Wigmore cheese (in one piece)

5 slices of Parma ham

3 Cox's apples

1 tablespoon sugar

20g butter

Selection of salad leaves and herbs

Marinade for foie gras:

50ml brandy

50ml ruby port

50ml dry Madeira

1/2 teaspoon mignonette white pepper

With a small sharp knife, skin and de-vein the foie gras. Lay it out in a stainless steel tray, then sprinkle the marinade over, cover with cling film, and leave overnight in a cool place.

Next day, line a small terrine mould with the sliced Parma ham, trim the Wigmore cheese of its rind and shape it to form a long baton to the length of the terrine mould.

Remove the cling film from the foie gras and place in a moderate oven (120ºC) for approximately five minutes; when it is starting to give up its fat and is warmed through, remove from the oven. Place half of the foie gras into the mould, then lay in the baton of cheese. Top with the

remaining foie gras and fold Parma ham over the top. Place a light weight on top and chill in the fridge. Leave for at least one day before serving.

When ready to serve, make spheres of apple using a small ball cutter. Heat a frying pan and add the sugar: when the sugar is caramelising add the apple balls. Coat the balls with caramel, add butter, and season. Shake together well and pour into a small bowl to cool. Keep the cooking juices.

To assemble, place a mixture of salad leaves and herbs in the centre of each plate. Place two slices of the terrine on top; garnish with the apple balls and a drizzle of the apple juices.

Ingredients:

4 x 250g tronçon of halibut
from a large fish

10 branches of dried fennel

1 large sprig of thyme

2 bay leaves

4 anchovies

1 tablespoon anchovy oil

4 strips of dried orange zest

200ml olive oil

2 star anise

Splash of Pernod

For the beurre blanc:

50g shallots, finely chopped

50ml white wine vinegar

50ml white wine

1 bay leaf

5 peppercorns crushed

250g cold unsalted butter, cubed

1 tablespoon cold water

For the clams:

50g sliced shallots

1 clove garlic crushed

100ml white wine

1 kg surf clams or cockles

1 tablespoon olive oil

For the red wine sauce:

500g fish carcasses
(sea bass or red mullet are best)

1 bottle of red wine

100g button mushrooms sliced

100g shallots sliced

50ml whipping cream

1 sprig each thyme and rosemary

1 dried orange zest

1 star anise

50g unsalted butter

300ml veal glaze

For the beurre blanc, combine the shallots, bay leaf, peppercorns, wine and vinegar in a small saucepan. Bring to the boil and reduce to a syrup. Remove from the heat, add cold water, then whisk in butter little by little to obtain an emulsion. Put through a fine chinois and season with salt. Keep just warm.

To prepare the clams, heat the olive oil in a heavy based saucepan. When hot, quickly add the shallots, garlic, wine and clams. Cover and cook briskly until the clams open: strain immediately into a colander and keep warm.

For the red wine sauce heat the shallots in 10g of butter. Add half the mushrooms and cook for three minutes, then add half the wine and reduce by two thirds. In a separate pan add the rest of the mushrooms and wine and again reduce by two thirds. Add the two reductions together, add cream, orange, thyme, star anise, rosemary, glaze and carcasses. Simmer for 20 minutes and pass through a chinois. Whisk in the rest of the butter and season.

To cook the halibut, mix the fennel, thyme, bay leaves, anchovies, orange zests and star anise in a roasting pan. Coat these with the two oils and the Pernod. Lay the tronçons on top, white skin uppermost and baste with the liquid in the pan. Roast in the oven at 200ºC, basting frequently, for approximately ten minutes. Remove from the oven and allow to rest in a warm place for five minutes. Serve on warmed plates with the two sauces, a scattering of clams, and the vegetables of your choice.

Tronçon of halibut roasted over aromats with clams and two sauces

Serves 4

Apricot Napoleon

Serves 4

Ingredients:

75g sugar

3 egg yolks

3 egg whites

30g sugar

300ml cream

500g fresh apricots

3 tablespoons water

Stone the apricots and place in a heavy-based saucepan. Add the water, cover, and steam until the apricots are soft. Purée in a blender and pass through a fine sieve.

Boil the 75g sugar to soft ball and gradually whisk onto the egg yolks: continue mixing until cool. Add the apricots to the egg yolk mixture.

Whisk the egg whites and 30g sugar to soft peaks. Fold the cream into the apricot mixture. Then fold in the meringue until it is well incorporated and smooth.

Place into a cling film lined tray approximately 2.5cm deep, and freeze. When completely frozen cut into 4cm circles (you will need three per person), keeping these frozen until ready to serve.

For the pineapple tuiles:

300g sugar

300ml water

1 large pineapple

Slice the pineapple horizontally into discs 2mm thick. Boil the sugar and water, place the pineapple into the syrup and remove from heat. Poach for 2 minutes, then lay out the coated discs on a silicon paper lined tray and place in a warm place to dry.

When dry, cook at 160°C for approximately 8 minutes until slightly coloured, then remove from the oven and allow to cool. Keep in an airtight container until needed.

To assemble, place a pineapple disc on each plate. Top with an apricot cylinder, then repeat twice more. Garnish with slices of fruit and mint leaves.

THE LANDMARK LONDON

Gary Klaner

Warm terrine of quail, black pudding and foie gras, bois boudrin dressing

Serves 15

Ingredients:

*12 jumbo quail breasts,
wing bone and skin removed*

300g black pudding, cut into 1cm dice

700g chicken

100ml egg white

600ml double cream

400g foie gras

1 head Savoy cabbage

50g chives, finely chopped

For the bois boudrin dressing:

25g chervil, finely chopped

25g tarragon, finely chopped

25g chives, finely chopped

25g parsley, finely chopped

150ml tomato ketchup

100ml red wine vinegar

250ml olive oil

400g shallots, finely chopped

Before preparing the terrine, first de-vein and shape the foie gras at room temperature into a roulade, the length of the terrine mould, using two layers of cling film. Refrigerate to set.

Remove the outer leaves of the cabbage and discard. Remove the remaining leaves, wash and blanch in boiling salted water and refresh in iced salted water. Drain, dry well on a clean cloth, and reserve.

Mince the chicken through a mincer using the fine cutting blade. Place the mince in a food processor and blend together with the egg white; remove the mixture and place in a bowl over a bath of iced water. Slowly add the double cream, beating in well using a wooden spoon or spatula. Pass the mousse through a medium drum sieve; add the chives and black pudding; season well.

Using three layers of cling film, line the terrine mould with the blanched cabbage leaves, slightly overlapping each other. Leave approximately 5cm overhang on either side of the mould.

Using a palette knife, spread a 1cm layer of mousse to cover the sides and bottom of the mould.

Place six quail breasts in the centre lengthways on top of the mousse, slightly overlapping each other. Season and cover the quail breasts with another layer of the mousse. Once the foie gras has set, remove the cling film, season, place lengthways in the centre of the terrine, and cover with mousse.

Repeat this process, ensuring that the mousse reaches the top lip of the terrine mould. Finally, fold over the blanched cabbage and cling film. Place a butter paper wrapper and lid on top of the mould.

When required, cook the terrine in a water bath with a piece of card under the mould. Cook at 110°C for approximately one hour. Once cooked, allow the terrine to rest for 15 minutes, then turn out of the mould, slice and serve warm as shown.

For the bois boudrin, combine all the ingredients in a bowl and leave for one hour at room temperature before using.

Roasted fillet of barramundi, cassoulet of beans and purple potato, sauce Jacqueline

Serves 5

Ingredients:

5 x 170g barramundi fillets, skin on, scaled and scored

50ml olive oil

70g fine beans, prepared, halved

70g mange tout, prepared, halved

150g fresh unshelled peas

250g purple truffle potatoes, whole

250g plum tomatoes, whole

40g butter, unsalted

50g shallots, finely chopped

10g flat parsley, picked, chopped

300ml vegetable stock

*70g haricot beans,
soaked in water for 24 hours*

For the courgette flower:

5 courgette flowers

125g white unpasteurised crabmeat

180g brioche crumbs

1 whole egg

4 drops Worcestershire sauce, to taste

20g chives, chopped

*30g finely chopped shallots,
cooked in butter*

For the sauce Jacqueline:

100g shallots, sliced

15g ginger, chopped

50g carrots, sliced

50g butter, unsalted

400ml carrot juice

300ml double cream

100ml Noilly Prat

100ml white wine

Sweat the shallots in half the butter until tender, then add the drained haricot beans. Cover with the vegetable stock and cook slowly for approximately one hour until the beans are tender. Drain and allow to cool.

Wash and cook the truffle potatoes in their skins from cold in salted water until tender; drain and cool. Once cold, peel and slice approximately 5mm thick and reserve. Cook the fine beans, fresh peas and sugar snap peas separately in boiling salted water; refresh in iced salted water, drain and reserve. Blanch the tomato in boiling salted water and refresh in iced salted water.

Remove the skin and seeds and cut the flesh into 1.5cm squares.

For the courgette flower, pick the white crabmeat, ensuring there is no shell. Mix with the cooked shallots, breadcrumbs, egg, and Worcester sauce; season. Very carefully, lightly wash and dry the courgettes and flowers, ensuring the flowers do not break off. Gently half fill each flower with the crabmeat mixture and fold the ends over to form a seal. Trim the end of the courgette at an angle and steam for six minutes.

Seal the seasoned barramundi skin side down until the skin is golden and finish cooking in the oven at 170°C for eight minutes.

For the sauce Jacqueline, sweat the shallots, carrots and ginger in 25g of butter with no colour until tender. Add the alcohol and reduce to a glaze. Add the carrot juice and reduce by a third. Add the double cream and cook slowly until the consistency of single cream is achieved; season. Allow to rest, then pass through a fine strainer. Whisk in the remaining butter before serving, and lightly foam with a hand blender.

To serve, reheat all the vegetables in a little butter and vegetable stock; season. Add the tomato dice and finish with the chopped flat parsley. Plate as shown.

Iced honey and granola parfait, gooseberry coulis

Serves 4-6

Ingredients:

1 egg

30g caster sugar

30g honey

1 leaf bronze gelatine

160ml double cream

80ml natural yoghurt

120g granola bar

Juice of half a lime

For the gooseberry coulis:

1kg frozen gooseberries

300g caster sugar

1 litre water

Juice of 1 lime

For the chocolate ganache:

160g chocolate couverture drops

85ml double cream

35g unsalted butter

For the chocolate ribbons:

200g dark chocolate couverture drops

For the sugar stick:

165g caster sugar

35ml water

5g glucose

Whisk the egg, sugar and honey in a bowl over boiling water, then whisk the mixture in a machine until it is cool and fluffy. Add the soaked, squeezed-out and melted gelatine.

Half whip the double cream and add the yoghurt; fold the egg and honey mixture into the cream/yoghurt mix, add the crumbled granola bar and finish with lime juice. Pour the mixture into a greaseproof paper-lined tray 2cm deep and freeze. When frozen cut to the required size and shape.

For the gooseberry coulis, place all the ingredients, except the lime juice, in a pan and simmer slowly until the fruit is tender, then take off the heat and allow to cool. When the mixture is cold, drain the gooseberries, and purée in a food processor. Finally, pass through a fine strainer and add the lime juice.

For the chocolate ganache, boil the cream, adding the chocolate when boiling, then add the butter. Cool on flat trays in the refrigerator, and form into an egg shape (quenelle) with two spoons.

To make the chocolate ribbons, temper the chocolate by melting it at 45°C. Remove half, and cool on a marble slab until it reaches 20°C, then add this back into the melted chocolate and melt again until the temperature is between 29°C and 31°C. If these temperatures are not accurate, you will notice marbled grey streaks in the chocolate. Pour the chocolate onto a tray at room temperature and spread out evenly. Pull a comb with approximately 5mm gaps through the chocolate and allow to set at room temperature. Once completely set, remove by scraping gently off with a metal scraper.

For the sugar stick, boil all the ingredients together to 160°C. Place the bottom of the pan directly into cold water to stop the sugar cooking any further. Allow the sugar to cool until it becomes pliable, then make your required sugar stick by spooning some of the sugar with a fork onto silicon paper and allowing it to set at room temperature. Store in an airtight container until required.

LEWTRENCHARD MANOR

Jason Hornbuckle

Tian of crab with sautéed scallops, coriander and a curry infused oil

Serves 4

Ingredients:

200g white crabmeat

2 tablespoons crème fraîche

4 beef tomatoes

2 cloves garlic, chopped

6 sprigs thyme, chopped

10 leaves basil, chopped

Juice of 2 lemons

2 tablespoons coriander, chopped

8 large fresh scallops

Virgin olive oil

Rock salt and cracked white pepper

Chervil to garnish

For the avocado purée:

2 ripe avocado

Juice of 1 lime

1/2 teaspoon ground cumin

For the curry and coriander oil:

1/4 teaspoon powdered turmeric

1 teaspoon coriander seeds

1 teaspoon white peppercorns

1 teaspoon mustard seeds

1 cinnamon stick

1/2 teaspoon ground fennel

4 cardamom pods

1 clove garlic, chopped

1 mild green chilli, deseeded and chopped

1 large bunch coriander

In a bowl, mix together the crabmeat, crème fraîche, chopped coriander, lemon juice, and salt and pepper to taste, and put to one side. Peel and deseed the tomatoes and cut them with a round cutter, then slice each tomato into two discs. Place these on a tray and marinade with rock salt, garlic, thyme, pepper, basil, and a drizzle of good olive oil. Leave to infuse for two to three hours.

To make the purée, peel the avocado and process in a blender until smooth. Add the lime juice and cumin; season to taste.

For the curry oil, place the coriander seeds, cumin seeds, white peppercorns, mustard seeds and cinnamon stick in a dry pan and lightly toast. Add the rest of the ingredients apart from the fresh coriander, cover with good virgin olive oil, and slowly heat for 30 minutes. Pass the liquid through muslin, then leave to cool for a short while. Pick the leaves from the coriander and blanch in boiling water for one second: refresh immediately in iced water, add to the oil, and blend the mix until it is a pale green. Season, and cool quickly in the fridge.

To serve, layer the round cutter used for the tomatoes: first a tomato disc, then the crabmeat, purée in the middle, crabmeat again, then a tomato disc on top. Season and rapidly caramelise the scallops in a hot pan, then place two on each plate with the infused oil, a sprinkling of rock salt and cracked pepper, and chervil to garnish.

Stuffed saddle of rabbit with basil, sunblushed tomato and smoked garlic mash

Serves 4

Ingredients:

2 saddles rabbit, including shoulder

100g sunblushed tomatoes

15 large basil leaves

1 egg

50ml cream

8 slices Parma ham

Caul fat for wrapping

Olive oil

For the sauce:

The bones from the rabbit

1 onion, chopped

2 carrots, chopped

1 head garlic

1/2 celeriac, chopped

10 button mushrooms

1 sprig thyme

1 sprig rosemary

2 bay leaves

10 white peppercorns

100ml white wine

50g tomato purée

For the mash:

6 peeled cloves of garlic

4 large King Edward potatoes

Olive oil

To garnish:

50g French beans

50g trumpet mushrooms

Bone out the saddle and shoulders. If the butcher is preparing the meat, ask to keep the bones. Put the shoulder meat in a blender with a little salt and blend until smooth. Add the basil, tomatoes, egg, and cream; blend until combined and season. Place this stuffing on the saddle and wrap the belly around, then roll first in the Parma ham, then in the caul. To help avoid tearing, soak the caul in warm salted water before using. Tie the parcels with string and leave in the fridge until required.

In a heavy bottomed pan sauté the bones in a little oil until browned, then remove the bones and gently caramelise the vegetables and herbs for the sauce. Return the bones, add the tomato purée, and cook for about five minutes, then add the wine and reduce by half. Add sufficient water to cover, then cook gently for four to five hours, skimming off the fat at regular intervals. Remove the bones and vegetables and pass the stock through a fine sieve into a clean pan, then reduce until it comes to a sauce consistency. Season to taste.

Smoke the garlic cloves by placing them on a cooling rack over oak wood chips and covering the rack with foil. Heat for an hour at 120°C, then leave to cool and purée the cloves. Cook and mash the potatoes, then blend in the olive oil and smoked garlic purée, seasoning to taste.

Roast the saddles in a little olive oil for five minutes at 180°C, then rest the meat. Blanch the French beans and sauté the trumpet mushrooms; place the mash in the centre of the plate. Remove the string and slice the saddles, and place on the potato with the beans, mushrooms, and sauce arranged around the plate.

Set lemon custard with raspberry ice cream and lemon curd

Serves 4

For the custard:

85ml lemon juice

30ml orange juice

3 eggs

2 egg yolks

125g sugar

175ml double cream

Demerara sugar

For the lemon curd:

380ml lemon juice

12 egg yolks

6 eggs

300g sugar

250g butter

Raspberry ice cream:

250ml milk

250ml double cream

50g sugar

8 egg yolks

1 tablespoon glucose

100g sugar

500g raspberry coulis

200ml crème de cassis

To garnish:

*12 thin round
lemon shortbread biscuits*

28 small fresh raspberries

4 mint leaves

4 biscuit baskets

To make the lemon custard, mix the egg yolks, eggs, and sugar in a bowl. Boil together the orange and lemon juices and the cream in a saucepan, then pour the hot liquid over the egg mixture and stir until the sugar has dissolved. Divide the mix into four demi-tasse cups and cook for 35-40 minutes at 110°C, then cool and refrigerate.

For the lemon curd, bring the lemon juice and sugar to the boil. Place the eggs and yolks in a large pan and whisk in the syrup, then return to the stove and slowly heat until the mixture thickens. Remove from the heat and slowly whisk in the butter, small cubes at a time. Leave in the fridge to set.

To prepare the raspberry ice cream, boil the milk, cream, glucose, and the 50g of sugar in a saucepan. Meanwhile, whisk the eggs, yolks, and 100g of sugar in a mixer until light and fluffy; add the cream mix and continue whisking until cool. Stir in the liqueur and coulis and leave to chill overnight, then churn until frozen in an ice cream machine.

To serve, caramelise the top of the custard with demerara sugar. Layer the lemon curd and raspberries between lemon shortbread biscuits and garnish with mint leaves. Put a scoop of ice cream in a basket on each plate (shown with an optional garnish of dark chocolate tuile and raspberry sorbet). Decorate the plate with raspberry coulis.

MALLORY COURT

Simon Haigh

Salad of Cornish lobster with avocado and mango

Salad of Cornish lobster with avocado and mango

Serves 4

Ingredients:

2 live lobsters apprx. 700g each

1 avocado

1 mango

Olive oil

Various salad leaves washed and picked

2 Granny Smith apples

1 cucumber

2 carrots

Peel and slice the avocado and mango. Liquidise the mango trimmings with a little olive oil to make a dressing for the salad. Scoop out the apples, cucumber, and carrots with a small parisienne scoop. Cook the carrots in boiling salted water, then leave to cool and reserve with the apple and cucumber.

Bring a large pan of water to a rapid boil and immerse the lobsters. Bring the water back to the boil for a further nine minutes, then take out the lobsters and put them in a bowl of iced water. Once cold, remove the tails and claws; crack the shells and extract the meat in whole pieces. Using one claw and half a tail per person, arrange the meat with the salad on the plate and dress with vinaigrette, positioning the avocado and mango around the lobster with the parisienne balls on top.

Loin of hare wrapped in cured ham with a peppery port sauce

Serves 4

Bring the St Emilion to the boil then leave to cool; meanwhile, remove the hare loins from the saddles and trim the meat. Chop the bones quite finely and cover both these and the loins with the wine, then leave overnight in the fridge to marinate.

Take out the meat and bones, setting the marinade aside. Wrap the loins in the ham. Roast the bones until coloured, then add the mirepoix of finely diced vegetables and cook out on the hob. Add the herbs, deglaze the pan with the sherry vinegar, then add the marinade wine and reduce by two thirds. Add the chicken stock and veal glace and reduce to the desired consistency, then pass twice, first through a fine chinois then through muslin. Make a reduction with the port and peppercorns, then add the strained sauce; taste and season.

Pan fry the loins wrapped in ham until nicely coloured, then cook in the oven at 180°C for around six minutes until the meat is pink throughout. Halve the wrapped loins on the diagonal and serve with the sauce and the vegetables of your choice.

Ingredients:

2 large hare saddles	500ml chicken stock
16 slices cured ham	200ml veal glace
1 bottle St Emilion	200ml port
I sprig thyme	Green peppercorns
1 bay leaf	200g mirepoix; leek, carrot, and onion
	100ml Sherry vinegar

Whole roast wax tip pear, almond butterscotch sauce

Serves 4

Ingredients:

4 firm pears

250ml stock syrup

Half a split vanilla pod

100g toasted almonds

Blackberries for garnish

Nougatine:

4 eggs

50g roasted flaked almonds

50g roasted hazelnuts

50g pistachio nuts

Seeds from 2 vanilla pods

20g honey

80g caster sugar

150g candied fruit

500ml double cream

4 circular brandy snaps

Butterscotch sauce:

500ml double cream

300g sugar

150g butter

Poach the pears in the stock syrup for twenty minutes, then chill and reserve. Meanwhile, prepare the butterscotch sauce by melting the butter and half the sugar, then add the cream and bring the liquid to the boil. In a separate pan heat the remaining sugar to caramel, then – carefully, as the combination will boil fairly rapidly – add the hot caramel to the butter and cream mix. Cool and reserve, adding a little water if the sauce is too thick.

To make the nougatine, whisk the eggs, sugar, honey and vanilla to ribbon stage, then continue whisking over a warm bain marie until light and fluffy. Leave to cool, then fold in the fruit and nuts. Whisk the cream to soft peak, then fold into the mixture.

Line a terrine with greaseproof paper and pour in the nougatine mix, then freeze. When the nougatine has frozen cut it into slices about half an inch thick, then shape these into discs; there should be around eight per terrine.

In a hot pan, lightly caramelise the pears in a knob of butter and a little sugar, then put them in the oven at 200°C for five minutes. Warm up some butterscotch sauce and add the toasted almonds. Place a nougatine disc on each plate under a brandy snap, then when the pear is ready sit it on top and pour over the butterscotch sauce. Garnish each plate with a few blackberries.

THE MARCLIFFE AT PITFODELS

Simon Gosling

Cappucino of crab and ginger bisque: tortellini of langoustines and basil

Serves 4

For the bisque:

1 large crab (steamed for 5 minutes)

50g clarified butter

1 tablespoon olive oil

1 medium onion

1 medium carrot

3 cloves garlic

1.25 litres chicken stock

60g tomato purée

2 plum tomatoes

2oz flour

6 black peppercorns

1/2 teaspoon fennel seeds

1/2 small chilli

1/2 packet dill weed

2 sprigs thyme

25g root ginger

100ml cognac

100ml Pernod

75ml white wine

Maldon sea salt

Cayenne pepper

Heat the olive oil and clarified butter in a thick bottomed pan until the butter has melted, then insert the crab and cook with the lid on for ten minutes. Make a mirepoix of the onion, carrot, ginger and thyme. Remove the lid and break up the crab with a rolling pin or other object heavy enough to smash the shell, then add the mirepoix and cook for a further five minutes.

Deglaze the pan with the cognac and Pernod, then flambé: add the tomato purée and cook it out. Stir in the flour to make a roux, adding the stock, chopped plum tomatoes, remaining herbs, spices, and dill weed. Season with sea salt and cayenne pepper to taste and let the bisque come to the boil; skim if required.

Simmer for an hour on a low heat, then extract and set aside the claws. Purée the remaining bisque in a liquidiser until smooth, then pass through a muslin to remove any shell. Add any final seasoning required and set aside.

For the tortellini filling:

6 basil leaves

*16 fresh langoustine tails
(8 for soup garnish)*

1 teaspoon freshly grated Parmesan

Half an egg white

Purée eight of the langoustine tails with the basil and Parmesan and stand in the fridge to chill. When chilled, beat in the egg white; check the seasoning, and return to the fridge.

For the pasta;

250g flour

3 egg yolks

2 whole eggs

1 tablespoon olive oil

1/4 teaspoon saffron powder

Salt

Mix all the ingredients together using a tough hook on a mixing machine to create a firm dough. Rest the dough in a plastic bag for two hours, then pin through a pasta machine until #7 in thickness: the thinner the pasta, the better the shape and texture of the tortellini. Cut off the edges and punch out eight 50mm discs.

Place a little of the langoustine mixture in the centre of each disc, then wet the rim of the discs with water and fold into crescent moons, pinching the edges together. Place in the fridge on a floured tray to dry.

When ready to serve, blanch the tortellini in salted water. Meanwhile in a hot pan sauté the remaining langoustine tails for two minutes on their backs only in a little olive oil; season. In four warm bowls, place the tortellini and langoustines and ladle in soup. Reserve and bamix a small amount of the soup to make a light froth: garnish with this and a little chopped dill.

Canon of roe deer with a potato, black pudding and shallot torte, asparagus mousse and sautéd chanterelles

Serves 4

For the canon of roe deer:

*Four 170g fillets of roe deer
(save the trimmings for the jus)*

1 chicken suprême

1 egg white

8 fine slices Parma ham

230g fresh chanterelles

500g chopped fresh flat parsley

1 pinch nutmeg

2 sprigs thyme

50g butter

300ml double cream

For the torte:

8 potatoes

340g butter

1 litre good chicken stock

1^1/$_2$ tablespoons olive oil

8 shallots

110g black pudding

For the mousse:

230g asparagus

1^1/$_2$ eggs

1^1/$_2$ egg yolks

150ml double cream

Half a clove garlic, crushed

100ml white wine

For the jus:

300ml game stock

300ml chicken stock

6 pimento berries, crushed

2 cloves

1 blade mace

2 bay leaves

50g butter

4 shallots, chopped

1 glass cabernet sauvignon

Roe deer trimmings

Heat the olive oil until smoking, then seal the roe deer fillets, season, and set on a plate to cool.

Blend the chicken breast, egg, and cream in a processor to form a mousse; season and place in a clean bowl in the fridge. Sauté three quarters of the chanterelles in butter, remove from the pan, chop finely and leave to cool. Finely chop the parsley and pick the thyme leaves; when the chanterelles are cold add them together with the herbs to the mousse. Check the seasoning.

Lay two slices of Parma ham on a piece of cling film and spread the mousse evenly over the ham. Place a fillet of roe deer on top and wrap the cling film tightly to form a sausage shape: repeat for all four fillets, wrap the sausages individually in foil for protection and store in the fridge until required.

Roast the canons in their foil in a moderate oven (170°C) for 15-20 minutes. Remove to a warm place to rest for ten minutes, then remove the foil and film and slice into three equal pieces.

To make the torte bring the butter and chicken stock to the boil in a pan, removing from the heat when they have emulsifed. Peel and wash the potatoes and cut into thinly sliced discs – as thin as possible – preferably with a mandolin. Toss the potato slices in the emulsified stock and place over heat for five minutes to wilt but not cook the slices. Peel, finely shred, and sauté the shallots in the olive oil until slightly coloured. Season well, drain in a colander and set aside.

Place an 8" flan ring on a baking sheet and arrange the sliced potatoes inside the flan ring, overlapping the lip. After two layers of potato, crumble the black pudding and spread it evenly over the potatoes; repeat with the sautéed shallots.

Finish with a layer of potatoes in a scalloped effect and season.

Transfer to a 150°C oven and cook for 40 minutes, pressing down every ten minutes to prevent burning. When cooked, remove from the oven, place a tray on top and lightly press the torte.

To prepare the mousse, peel the asparagus and blanch in boiling water for four minutes, then remove and refresh in iced water to retain the colour. Heat the cream with the garlic and white wine, then place asparagus and cream in a liquidiser and purée until smooth. Pass through a sieve into a clean bowl, then add the egg and whisk, checking the seasoning.

To make the jus, sauté the shallots and trimmings in the butter to a deep brown colour. Add the pimento berries, mace, and cloves. Deglaze the pan with the wine and reduce to a syrupy consistency. Add both stocks and bring to the boil; skim, and add the bay leaves. Reduce the stock to a third, season, pass through a muslim cloth, and place in a clean pan ready to serve.

To serve, arrange the canons of roe deer on a plate with the torte and the mousse as shown: drizzle with the jus.

Tian of white chocolate, lemon ganache, fresh raspberries and fruit granité

Serves 4

For the ganache cream:

50g butter

125g icing sugar

2 egg yolks

20g kirsch

20g lemon juice

Zest of 2 lemons

150g white chocolate

190g whipped cream

Cream the butter and icing sugar, then beat in the eggs one at a time making sure the mixture doesn't curdle. Warm the kirsch, lemon juice and zest together, and beat slowly, a little at a time, into the butter mixture until it is all absorbed. Melt the white chocolate over a bain marie and beat most of it into the mix, then fold in the whipped cream. When fully dissolved, put in the freezer to chill for five minutes, then place in the fridge ready for use.

Form four cylinders of the lemon chocolate mix topped with discs of a slightly greater diameter. Use any excess cream for decoration.

For the raspberry coulis:

2 punnets of fresh raspberries

2 dessert spoons of sugar

Juice of 1 lemon

Place all the ingredients in a pan and heat until the sugar is dissolved, but do not boil. Blend in a processor, then pass through a fine mesh strainer.

For the granité:

8 passion fruit, pulped

1 litre orange juice

Juice of 1 lemon

200ml vodka

125g sugar

Place all the ingredients in a pan and bring to the boil, then transfer the liquid to a shallow tray and freeze it down. When frozen, fluff up using a fork whisk. The iced granité is now ready to serve.

MASTER BUILDER'S HOUSE HOTEL

Denis Rhoden

Salmon terrine with white bean dressing

Serves 6

Ingredients:

1/4 side of salmon

1 sheet nori

1 pinch wasabi

1 pinch sea salt

For the dressing:

50g haricots blanc
soaked in water for 24 hours

500ml ham (or chicken) stock

Half a head of garlic

1 red pepper, finely diced

1 teaspoon thyme leaves

1 red onion, finely chopped

75ml olive oil

6 teaspoons aged balsamic vinegar

Season the salmon with salt and wasabi, then place on the nori and roll. Wrap the cylinder tightly in cling film, then cook in the film for 30 minutes at 70°C. Allow, to cool, slice into portions and remove the film.

For the dressing, cook the soaked and drained haricots in the stock with the garlic until they are soft. Strain, add the rest of the ingredients while the beans are still hot, then arrange the dressing around the terrine on the plate.

Roast lobster with orange and sesame dressing

Serves 4

Ingredients:

4 x 500g lobsters
Olive oil

For the dressing:

4 oranges, segmented and diced
4 teaspoons sesame seeds
4 tablespoons sesame oil

Lobster biscuits:

14g flour
8g sugar
2g sea salt
20g butter
10g egg white
2g lobster coral
1g fresh coriander, chopped

Kill the lobsters by inserting a sharp knife between the eyes, then place in an oven pan, coat with olive oil, and roast for twelve minutes at 170°C. Allow to cool, then remove the tail and claw meat.

For the lobster biscuits, mix all the ingredients together and spread the mix thinly on a baking tray, then bake for five minutes at 160°C. Prepare the dressing by reducing the orange juice by half, then add the diced oranges, sesame seeds and oil, and remove from the heat, stirring to emulsify.

Hazelnut chocolate ganache with kumquat compote

Makes 10 portions

Ganache:

300g hazelnut chocolate

300g whipping cream

Japonnais biscuit:

100g egg white

125g sugar

125g ground hazelnuts

Boil the cream and pour over the chocolate, whisking until it lightens in colour.

Whisk together the egg whites and sugar until they form a pale meringue, then fold in the hazelnuts. Spread the mix thinly on a baking sheet and bake for five minutes at 170°C then leave to cool, cutting the biscuit into strips while still warm.

Layer a terrine mould with alternate layers of Japonnais and ganache until it is full, then smooth the top of the mould and leave in the fridge ready to serve.

Kumquat compote:

200g kumquats

200g sugar

250g water

1 vanilla pod

Boil all the ingredients together until the sauce thickens, then remove the vanilla pod and set aside ready for serving.

THE MILLENNIUM BAILEY'S HOTEL

Luca Ciano

Roast seabass with a ravioli of langoustine and amaretto, shellfish sauce and saffron oil

Serves 4

Ingredients:

4 x 150 gms seabass delice

1 kg fresh langoustine blanched and peeled (save the shells)

100g shaved fennel

50ml saffron oil

100g deep fried leek

Sea salt and milled pepper

75g mirepoix (roughly cut fennel, leek, carrot, celery, and onion)

25ml olive oil

2 sprigs thyme

1 bay leaf

6 peppercorns

2 cloves garlic

1 shot brandy

1 shot Pernod

250ml double cream

1 tablespoon tomato purée

100ml fish stock

For the pasta:

60g '00' soft flour

1 egg

1 egg yolk

Pinch of salt and pepper

10g saffron pistils

Ravioli filling:

12 langoustine tails

3 crushed amaretto biscuits

15g shallots, finely chopped

1 small clove garlic, crushed

1 shot brandy

30ml double cream

To make the pasta, make a hollow in the flour. Whisk the other ingredients together and slowly fold into the flour. Knead into a firm dough and allow to rest for two to three hours tightly wrapped in cling film. Roll out the pasta, either in a machine or with a rolling pin, and cut out eight discs of approximately 8cm diameter for the ravioli.

Sauté without colouring the shallots and garlic, then deglaze the pan with brandy and reduce. Blanch and add the langoustine tails with the amaretto biscuit and bind with a little cream: correct the seasoning and chill. Divide the mix onto the pasta discs, fold in half, and seal the ravioli with water, avoid creases and air pockets. Cook for five minutes in boiling salted water with a touch of oil, then drain and keep to one side.

To prepare the shellfish sauce, heat the olive oil in a thick bottomed pan and when smoking add the langoustine shells; sauté for a couple of minutes, then add the mirepoix, thyme, bayleaf, and garlic. Continue cooking, adding a spoon of tomato purée, then deglaze the pan with the brandy and pernod. Reduce by half, add the fish stock and reduce again. Add the cream and cook quickly to a sauce consistency; correct the seasoning and pass through a fine sieve.

To serve, season the skin side of the seabass and seal until crispy, then cook for ten minutes at 180°C. Deep fry and dry the shredded leek, cook the fennel shavings in a little butter and vegetable stock until soft, then place the seabass on the fennel with the ravioli on top and the deep fried leek above. Arrange three langoustine tails on each plate, and complete by drizzling around the shellfish sauce and saffron oil.

Venison tagliata with grilled vegetables, rocket and balsamic reduction

Serves 4

Ingredients:

500g cleaned venison loin

4 baby aubergines

4 baby courgettes

2 baby red peppers

2 baby yellow peppers

2 heads baby fennel

1 bunch baby carrots

50g wild rocket leaves

50g shaved reggiano Parmesan

25g sea salt

Freshly milled pepper

Marinade for venison and vegetables:

250ml olive oil

3 cloves garlic

2 sprigs rosemary

2 sprigs thyme

6 leaves sage

6 black peppercorns

2 bayleaves

For the dressing:

50ml reduced Modena balsamic vinegar

100ml good quality Italian olive oil

Mix the marinade and immerse the meat, leaving to infuse for at least 24 hours. Prepare and grill the vegetables and add to the venison to marinate overnight.

Remove the venison from the marinade, pat dry, season with salt and pepper and seal all over in a hot griddle pan. Roll the meat tightly in cling film and chill in the fridge for two hours, then slice into an even number of slices for serving (minimum 16). Position the venison and vegetables on the plate and flash heat them under a hot salamander or high grill. Dress and arrange the rocket leaves on the plate with the Parmesan shavings; decorate the plate with balsamic reduction and olive oil

Caramelised honey and chilli pineapple with a white chocolate saffron brûlée

Serves 6

Saffron brûlée:

500ml double cream

$1/4$ vanilla pod, split

4 egg yolks

2 whole eggs

100g caster sugar

5g saffron pistils

25g white chocolate

Blend the eggs, sugar, and saffron in a bowl. Warm together the cream and the vanilla pod without boiling, then pour onto the egg mix, adding the chocolate at the same time, and whisk until cool. Leave to infuse for one hour, then pour into earthenware dishes and cook in a bain marie at 120°C for 45 minutes. Allow to cool and set in the fridge overnight.

Croquant tower:

200g toasted flaked almonds

200g granulated sugar

Preheat a stainless steel saucepan: when hot slowly add the sugar, adding more as it dissolves and browns. When it is completely dissolved add the almonds, coating them in the caramel, then pour the mix immediately onto a tray lined with silicon paper and allow to cool. When cold, break into pieces and grind the chunks to a fine grain in a food processor. Sprinkle this onto a tray lined with silicone paper and place in the oven at 200°C until completely melted, then remove from the oven, cover with another sheet of silicon, and carefully roll with a rolling pin until a thin layer is formed.

When cooled take off the top layer of silicon and replace in the oven for two to three minutes, then using a large lightly oiled knife cut into rectangles 85 x 55mm. As the croquant hardens roll it around a lightly oiled whisk handle or similar to shape into tubes, and allow to cool.

Pineapple crisp and chilli pineapple:

1 supersweet pineapple

100g sugar

200g water

200g clear honey

$1/2$ chopped red chilli

2 oranges segmented

Boil together the sugar and water. Top and tail the pineapple and cut out six horizontal discs of around 2-3mm thickness. Pass the slices through the boiling sugar and water, then place them on a tray lined with silicon paper and dry in the oven overnight at 80°C. Before removing increase the oven temperature to 200°C and crisp the pineapple until it is golden brown.

Remove the skin from the remainder of the pineapple and slice to a thickness of around 1cm. Preheat a griddle pan and caramelize the pineapple on both sides: no fat or oil is required. Finally, heat the honey and chilli together on a high heat for two to three minutes, add the orange segments, and set aside.

To serve, scoop out one ball of the brûlée mix per serving with an ice cream scoop, dusting the balls with icing sugar and glazing with a blowtorch. Place the remaining mix in a piping bag with a $1/4$" plain nozzle. Glue a croquant tower to each plate with a little caramel, then fill the tower with brûlée mix. Lay the pineapple crisp on top, securing with a little of the brûlée mix, and place a slice of warm pineapple onto the plate dressed with the honey and chilli syrup. Sit the ball of brûlée onto the pineapple crisp and serve.

Gary Lissemore

Warm salad of wild mushroom, white asparagus, pancetta and Parmesan with balsamic vinegar

Serves 4

Ingredients:

*300g mixed wild mushrooms:
eg shiitake; morel; oyster; chestnut*

*140g mixed leaf: wild rocket; frisée;
dandelion leaves; chicory*

50g pancetta lardons

1 bunch (12 pieces) white asparagus

50g fresh Parmesan

10ml balsamic vinegar

Wash and pick the leaves and allow to drain. Pick the stalks from the mushrooms; do not wash, but rub off any dirt with a damp cloth. Blanch the asparagus in salted boiling water until tender – around three minutes. In a preheated frying pan heat the pancetta lardons until crisp, then place on kitchen towels to drain off the fat.

Dress the leaves in the centre of the plate, then sprinkle with the pancetta. Put the mushrooms in a heated pan with a drizzle of olive oil and cook for two minutes, then add the balsamic vinegar and cook for a further minute. Serve the mushrooms on top of the leaves, topped with the grated Parmesan and asparagus.

Szechuan orange duck breast with rosemary roasted Jersey Royals, baby beetroot and spring greens

Serves 4

Ingredients:

*4 large duck breasts,
skinned and boned*

1 tablespoon olive oil

140g baby beetroot

1 tablespoon clear honey

1 tablespoon hoi sin sauce

140g spring greens/pak choi

1 tablespoon light soy sauce

1 tablespoon dark soy sauce

200g Jersey Royals

1 sprig rosemary

For the marinade:

1 tablespoon szechuan peppercorns

1 tablespoon garam masala

*1 teaspoon each of sesame seed oil,
wasabi paste, ground ginger,
coriander seed*

Zest and juice of 1 orange

2 tablespoons sake

1 tablespoon clear honey

For the sauce:

1 tablespoon hoi sin sauce

1 tablespoon fresh ginger, grated

Zest and juice of 1 orange

1 tablespoon fresh coriander, chopped

With a sharp knife score both sides of the duck breasts to let the marinade infuse. Mix together the marinade ingredients, rub into the duck, then place the breasts in the fridge for at least two hours.

To prepare the sauce, liquidise all the ingredients until smooth, then pass through a fine sieve and set to one side. If the result is thicker than desired, dilute with a tablespoon of water.

Preheat the oven to 200°C. Parboil the potatoes, then roast with the rosemary for 20 – 25 minutes. While the potatoes are roasting, heat a non stick frying pan and sauté the beetroot until golden brown. In another pan, sear the duck breasts for one to two minutes on both sides; when golden add to the beetroot, drizzle with honey, and cook for a further four to five minutes until the meat is pink. Meanwhile, cook the greens in a wok with the light soy sauce until tender – about three minutes – then drain.

To serve, place potatoes in the centre of the plate with greens on top and the baby beetroot around them. Arrange the duck breast, sliced into three, on top of the greens. Sprinkle a few drops of the dark soy sauce on the side.

Lemon grass and coconut ice cream

Serves 4

Ingredients:

200ml double cream

100ml milk

500ml coconut milk

1 vanilla pod

6 lemon grass sticks

6 egg yolks

100g sugar

3 tablespoons crème fraîche

1 baby pineapple, peeled and sliced

1 mango, peeled and sliced

1 tablespoon clear honey

25g butter

To make the ice cream, warm together the milk, cream, coconut milk, vanilla pod and lemon grass in a thick bottomed pan for 15 minutes. Add the sugar to the egg yolks and beat until white, then add to the milk mix and stir over a low heat for six to eight minutes until it is a thick custard consistency. Extract the lemon grass and vanilla pod, and add the crème fraîche. Pour into an ice cream machine and churn until set.

Melt the butter in a non stick pan, then add the pineapple and mango. Drizzle with honey and cook for four to five minutes until golden brown. To serve, arrange the mango and pineapple on the plate as shown with a large scoop of ice cream on top.

NEWICK PARK

Mark Taylor

Salmon ceviche, avocado ice cream and oyster beignets

Serves 4

Ingredients:

350g raw salmon, sliced on an angle

4 teaspoons spring onions, sliced on an angle

4 teaspoons olive oil

4 teaspoons coriander, sliced

1 1/2 teaspoons red chilli, chopped

4 teaspoon diced tomato, skin and seeds removed

Juice of 2 limes

Salt, pepper and sugar to taste

For the ice cream:

450g caster sugar

400ml medium white wine

75g glucose

400ml water

8 ripe avocados

Juice of 4 lemons

400ml milk

For the beignets:

12 rock oysters, taken from the shell

450g tempura flour

Vegetable oil

For the lemon crème fraîche:

400g crème fraîche

Juice of 2 lemons

Curly endive lettuce to garnish

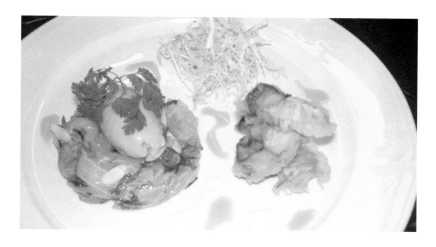

To make the ice cream, dissolve the sugar, wine, glucose and water in a saucepan over a low heat, then leave aside to cool. When cool, put into a food processor with the avocado and lemon juice and purée until you have a smooth paste. Evenly mix in the milk, then place into an ice cream machine and churn until frozen. Store in a sealed plastic container in the freezer until required.

Next place all the ingredients for the ceviche into a bowl and mix them together thoroughly. Allow all the flavours to infuse for at least 15 minutes, checking for seasoning and adjusting if necessary.

Place the tempura flour into a bowl and mix to a smooth paste with the water, then season. Use more water if needed to keep the batter thin enough to properly coat the oysters. Once the oysters have been removed from their shells, wash them well and place them on kitchen towel to drain, then dip them in the tempura batter and drop them one at a time into a fryer or deep pan of hot vegetable oil. Cook for two to three minutes until crisp, then lay out on kitchen paper to absorb any excess oil and set aside somewhere warm until ready to serve.

Mix the crème fraîche with the lemon juice and seasoning. Place in the fridge. Dress the curly endive with a little olive oil, lemon juice and salt and pepper.

To assemble the dish, place a 3" diameter pastry cutter towards the front of a large plate and carefully arrange the salmon slices within the cutter. Using the dressed curly endive, make a small ball of salad with your hands and place it at the top of the plate. Arrange the oyster beignets on top of each other to the side of the ceviche. Quenelle the avocado ice cream with a warmed dessert spoon and place the quenelle on top of the ceviche. Remove the cutter and drizzle the lemon crème fraîche around the rest of the plate.

Spiced butternut squash risotto with coriander oil

Serves 4

Ingredients:

1 butternut squash,
peeled and diced to 2cm

$^1/_2$ pinch cloves

$^1/_2$ cinnamon stick, broken up

1 pinch cardamon

1 pinch star anise

1 pinch cumin seeds

1 tablespoon brown sugar

50g butter, melted

1 litre vegetable stock

500g arborio rice

3 banana shallots, finely diced

1 clove garlic, crushed

Coriander oil:

1 bunch coriander, leaves picked

100ml vegetable oil

Red pepper reduction

3 red peppers

$^1/_2$ tablespoon sugar

Prepare an ice bath. Blanch the picked coriander leaves for 1 minute, plunge into the iced water, then drain thoroughly. Blend the leaves in a food processor with the vegetable oil for 5 minutes or until the oil is bright green in colour. Place in a container and put in the fridge to infuse overnight. Put muslin into a strainer and pour the oil mix into it, then allow the oil to drain for about two to three hours: do not squeeze it through as this will make it go cloudy. Store the coriander oil in a jar in the fridge until needed.

Place the squash, spices and butter on an oven tray and mix together well, then cook in a preheated oven at 200°C, for about 10-15 minutes until the squash is golden brown and soft. Meanwhile, bring the vegetable stock with the trimmings left over from dicing the squash to the boil. Simmer until the trimmings are cooked through, blend with a hand blender, and season the stock.

To make the risotto, sweat off the shallots and garlic in a little olive oil. Add the aborio rice and cook, stirring all the time for two to three minutes, until the rice is without colour. Add the stock a little at a time until it is almost completely absorbed by the rice, which should still have a bite once cooked. Finish off with a tablespoon of butter well mixed in.

For the pepper reduction, cut off the stalks and de-seed the peppers. Chop the flesh up into small pieces and purée with enough water to get the peppers moving in a blender until smooth. Place all the pulp into muslin and squeeze out the red liquid: reserve the liquid and throw away the pulp. Put the liquid in a pan with the sugar over a medium heat and reduce to a thick consistency. Allow the reduction to cool and store in the fridge until needed.

When everything is prepared, place a 4" cutter in the centre of a large main course bowl. Spoon the risotto into the cutter, to the rim, then place the roasted spiced squash on top, finishing the dish with coriander oil and the pepper reduction.

Warm chocolate fondant with marshmallow ice cream

Serves 4

Pink marshmallows:

450ml egg whites

450ml sugar

9 leaves of gelatine

2 pipettes of marshmallow essence

Red food colouring

Ice cream:

450ml milk

450ml cream

400g caster sugar

12 egg yolks

For the chocolate tuiles:

12 egg whites

500g icing sugar

200g plain flour

50g cocoa powder

500g melted butter, cooled

Dried banana slices:

1 green banana, thinly sliced

Stock syrup

Seeds from 1 vanilla pod

Lemon juice

Fondant:

135g plain or milk chocolate

125g unsalted butter

4 eggs

125g caster sugar

145g plain flour

25g coffee

50g white chocolate chunks

If not using bought ones, prepare the marshmallows. Place the sugar with a little water to dissolve it in a saucepan on a high heat and boil until it gets to 121°C, then take it off the heat to cool slightly. Meanwhile have the gelatine soaking in cold water until soft, and the egg whites whipping. Add the soaked gelatine to the warm sugar syrup, then when the eggs are fully whipped slowly pour in the sugar and gelatine syrup whilst the machine is still going. Add the marshmallow essence to taste and enough colouring to just turn pink, then place the meringue mixture into a piping bag with a half inch plain nozzle. Line a tray with silicon paper and cornflour, and pipe the mixture in a long straight line. Place in the fridge to set for about half an hour, then cut into small pieces with a warmed knife.

For the ice cream, whisk the yolks and sugar to a sabayon, while boiling the cream and milk together. Pour this into the sabayon in the mixing machine and continue mixing until cold. Churn the mix in an ice cream machine; just before it is set, add the chopped marshmallows and churn a little more. Take out of machine, place in a container and store in the freezer.

For the chocolate tuiles, start by breaking down the egg whites with a fork. Sift the icing sugar and flour together, mix in the cocoa powder, then mix all the ingredients together by hand. Make a triangle shaped stencil template out of a piece of plastic, ie the lid from a container. Spread the mixture thinly and smoothly over the template, then remove the template and bake in the oven at 180°C for five to six minutes. Carefully peel off the tuile and place it over a rolling pin to cool: it will be soft when it comes out of the oven, but will crispen on drying.

For the dried banana slices, slice the bananas lengthways, preferably with a mandolin to achieve slices of even thickness. Dip the slices immediately first in lemon juice then in the stock syrup: shake off any excess liquid. Place the slices on a tray lined with a silpat mat or silicon sheet and place in an oven on the lowest setting for at least two hours. Remove from the oven and shape the slices as required: they will crisp up very quickly.

Finally, prepare the chocolate fondants by melting the chocolate and butter together over a bain-marie, then away from the heat source gradually adding the eggs then the sugar.

Fold in the rest of the ingredients and pour the mixture into dariole moulds which have been lined with butter, then a mixture of the flour and sugar. Bake in the oven at 200°C for about 10 minutes, when they should be set on the outside but still liquid in the middle.

To assemble the dish, place the fondant on the plate with a banana slice inserted in the top. Next to that position the chocolate tuile, using a little sauce to stick it to the plate. Ball some of the ice cream onto the tuile. Garnish with puddles of raspberry coulis at the front of the plate and a sprig of mint on the ice cream.

OLD COURSE HOTEL

David Kinnes

Breast of quail, red chard, black pudding, roasted hazelnuts, pancetta, beetroot dressing

Serves 4

Ingredients:

4 quail

50g red chard

50g mini black pudding

25g whole shelled hazelnuts

75g pancetta, whole

50g cooked beetroot

100ml olive oil

Trim the breasts from the quail, removing any excess fat, trimming the wing bone and chining the knuckle at the top of the bone. Wash the red chard.

Chop the pancetta into lardons and fry in a non-stick pan until crisp, then drain on paper towels. Roast the hazelnuts for five to ten minutes at 150°C until evenly browned, then allow to cool. Dice the beetroot and combine with the olive oil.

Fry the quail breasts for about two minutes each side, then remove from the pan and replace with the black pudding cut into twelve slices. Heat the pudding for two minutes each side then place on paper towels.

To serve, arrange the chard in the centre of the bowl with a plain cutter, mixing in the hazelnuts and pancetta. Place the black pudding around the leaves, then sit the breast on top with beetroot dressing around the bowl.

Roast fillet of turbot, soft herb and lobster risotto, curry oil and aged balsamico

Serves 4

Ingredients:

700g turbot fillet

2 medium shallots

250g risotto rice

100ml shellfish (or fish) stock

5g each tarragon and dill, finely chopped

10g mascarpone cheese

25g butter

50g lobster meat

2ml curry oil

10ml aged balsamic vinegar

Skin and trim the turbot, then divide the fillet into four portions and set aside.

Finely chop and sauté the shallots in the butter in a saucepan, then add and season the risotto rice. Add the shellfish stock – use fish stock if completely unobtainable – bring the liquid to the boil and remove from the heat. Cover the pan with cling film and agitate at regular intervals until the rice has absorbed all the liquid, then add the mascarpone, lobster, and herbs, keeping a little back for garnish. Season to taste.

Roast the turbot fillets in a preheated oven pan for around three minutes per side until cooked through, then season and set aside to rest for two minutes. Place the risotto in the centre of each bowl, with a portion of fillet on top. Gently pour the curry oil around the turbot, followed by a few drops of the balsamic vinegar. In a bowl, coat the herbs kept back for garnish in curry oil, then arrange on the dish and serve.

Hot chocolate fondant, banana ice cream, praline crisp

Serves 4

Banana ice cream:

2 bananas, mashed

Juice of 1 lemon

500ml full cream milk

6 egg yolks

125g sugar

Half a vanilla pod

Put the milk in a pan, split the vanilla pod and scrape the seeds into the milk, then bring the milk to the boil. Meanwhile whisk the egg yolks and sugar until the mix is pale cream, then pour in half the milk, mix well, and add the mix back into the rest of the milk. Gently heat, stirring continually, and as soon as the custard coats the back of a spoon remove from the heat. Do not overcook at this stage as it will cause the custard to separate. When cool, add the bananas and lemon juice and store in the freezer in a shallow container stirring at least three times before it is frozen, or churn in an ice cream machine.

Chocolate fondant:

5 whole eggs

5 egg yolks

125g caster sugar

250g good quality dark chocolate

50g plain four, sieved

250g butter

Whisk the eggs, yolks, and sugar to ribbon stage, ideally with a hand blender. Melt the butter, chop the chocolate into small pieces and stir into the butter until completely integrated, then fold into the egg and sugar mix. Finally, fold in the flour until all the ingredients are smoothly incorporated, then spoon into moulds lined with butter and sugar. Bake for about seven minutes at 180°C: the centre should still be runny.

Praline crisp:

250g granulated sugar

200g flaked almonds

Toast the almonds on a tray in the oven at 200°C until golden brown. Place the sugar with a little water in a heavy based pan and cook to a caramel, then add and coat the almonds and pour the mix onto oiled greaseproof paper. Leave to go cold, then break up into small chunks and pulverise to a powder in a processor. Spread the powder thinly onto greaseproof or silicone paper and return to the oven at 200°C until the layer of praline is soft. Cut the praline into triangles, then drape the cut shapes over a rolling pin or other curved surface to become crisp as they cool.

To assemble the dish, place a praline crisp on the plate. Carefully turn the fondant out from the mould onto the crisp, then scoop a ball of ice cream on top of the fondant: may also be accompanied by vanilla sauce as shown here.

LE POUSSIN AT PARKHILL

Alex Aitken

Lobster and pearl barley risotto

Serves 4

From my Scottish roots – an uncle was a lobster fisherman on the East Coast at the little village of Dunbar – this dish uses that great Scottish grain, pearl barley.

Ingredients:

*1 cooked lobster,
diced into large chunks*

100g peas

100g broad beans, blanched and peeled of the tough outer skins

300g pearl barley, soaked overnight

2 shallots, finely chopped

1 clove garlic, crushed

1 teaspoon saffron

1 glass white wine

250ml fish or vegetable stock

250g Parmesan cheese

Mixed herbs

4 egg yolks

100g breadcrumbs

For the Parmesan crisps, spread finely grated Parmesan into four circles on baking sheets and bake until golden brown (keep back a little of the cheese for thickening the risotto). Allow the crisps to cool and they will easily slip off the tray.

Deep fried egg yolks are a delicate operation, but well worth the effort. First separate the yolks and very lightly poach them in boiling water, then plunge them into iced water. Dip the yolks in a flour and egg wash, coat with breadcrumbs, then deep fry.

To prepare the risotto, sweat the shallots and garlic until soft in a little olive oil and butter. Add the pearl barley and saffron, stirring to coat the grains in the fats. Add the white wine and reduce. Then add the stock and cook gently, seasoning to taste until the barley is tender. At the last minute add the diced lobster, peas, and broad beans; thicken with a little freshly grated parmesan.

To finish the dish use a pastry cutter or ring mould and press the risotto firmly down; top with Parmesan crisp and a herb salad, and finally with the deep fried egg.

Roast quail breast on a cabbage confit with crisp potato galette, surrounded by lightly cooked wild fungi

Serves 4

Le Poussin is renowned for using wild regional produce, much of it foraged by Caroline, wife of chef patron Alex Aitken. Especially mushrooms from the area of the New Forest where Le Poussin at Parkhill is situated.

Ingredients:

4 plump quail

2 large baking potatoes, shredded into thin strips

1 Savoy cabbage

1 glass white wine vinegar

1 teaspoon sugar

500g mixed wild mushrooms

1 bunch chives, chopped

2 plum tomatoes, peeled, deseeded and diced

Butter

Olive oil

The potato galettes can be prepared in advance. First squeeze out any excess water from the potato strips, then pour 200g of melted butter over the potato and season with salt and pepper. Cook in a little oil and butter until golden brown and dry on kitchen paper.

If they have not already been removed, take off the wishbones and wing bones before roasting the quail. Season well with salt and pepper and spread a thick layer of butter on the breasts, then brown in a frying pan for two minutes on each side. Roast in a hot oven – 180°C to 200°C – for four minutes breast up and four minutes breast down, then rest for at least ten minutes. Carefully remove the legs first, jointing them at the thigh and removing the meat from the thigh to leave the drumstick. Then remove the breasts.

For the cabbage confit, finely shred and cook the cabbage in a little butter until softened, then add the glass of white wine vinegar and the teaspoon of sugar and cook until the liquid has completely reduced.

To prepare the wild mushrooms, carefully clean and either break with the fingers or cut them into attractive bite size pieces. Toss the mushrooms in a little butter and olive oil to cook lightly, then add the diced tomato and chopped chives and season to taste.

To serve place a spoonful of cabbage confit in the centre topped with a potato galette, onto which go the breasts of quail. Spoon the mushroom mix around mingled with the drumsticks and thigh meat. Finish with the cooking juices and a drizzle of olive oil.

Apple dessert

Serves 4

We have our own little orchard at Parkhill: this dish uses apples to the full, contrasting flavours, temperatures, and texture.

Apple sorbet:

*250g Granny Smiths,
cored but not peeled*

75g icing sugar

Juice of 1 lemon

To preserve the fresh green colour of this sorbet, have all the ingredients ready and work quickly. First squeeze the lemon and have the juice ready. Add the apples and icing sugar and liquidise to a very fine purée. Finally pass through a fine mesh sieve and freeze, preferably in a sorbetière: store in cone shaped moulds. To garnish cut very thin slices of apple, brush with lemon juice, dust with icing sugar, and dry to apple crisps in a low oven

Calvados pannacotta:

1.5 litres double cream

70g caster sugar

1 stick cinnamon

1 small shot calvados

2 leaves gelatine

Bring the double cream, sugar and cinnamon to the boil and allow to infuse. Soften the gelatine leaves in a little cold water and add to the cream mix along with the calvados. Strain the mix into a mixing bowl and allow to cool, whisking periodically as the liquid cools. When almost set transfer into moulds and set in the fridge.

Caramelised apple millefeuille:

250g puff pastry

Icing sugar for dusting

*6 Granny Smith apples,
peeled, cored, and cut into fat slices*

*100ml whipped cream
or crème patissière*

20g butter

100g sugar

Roll out the puff pastry very thinly, dust with icing sugar, then roll up into a tight cylinder and chill. When chilled cut thin round slices from the cylinder, roll these out again, and cut out discs of pastry. Bake these between two baking sheets lined with sheets of parchment paper.

To caramelise the apples melt the butter in a thick bottomed pan, add the sugar and apples and turn them as they cook to a rich golden brown. Assemble with a disc of pastry, then whipped cream or crème patissière, another pastry layer, the caramelised apple, and a final roof of pastry.

To finish the dish drizzle three lines of caramel sauce and arrange the three apple flavours and textures.

POWDERMILLS HOTEL
& THE ORANGERY RESTAURANT

James Penn

Carpaccio of roasted apricot and ginger duck, sweet yellow pepper sorbet and honey biscuit

Serves 4

For the duck carpaccio:

1 Gressingham duck breast

100g dried apricots

1 stem ginger and syrup

3 tablespoons maple syrup

3 tablespoons olive oil

1 sprig thyme

8 sprigs chive (for garnish)

For the sorbet:

375g caster sugar

325ml water

45g glucose syrup

375ml pulped yellow pepper

Galliano

For the honey biscuit:

55g plain flour

55g honey

55g butter

1¹/2 egg whites

Trim the duck breast of any fat, then make an incision in the flesh to act as a pocket. Soften the dried apricots in hot water, strain, then mix them in a blender with the stem ginger, 1 tablespoon of the maple syrup, thyme, and a pinch of salt and pepper to a paste. Using a piping bag fill the duck breast, sealing the opening tightly with string. Marinate the stuffed breast in the olive oil, ginger syrup, and the remainder of the maple syrup for 8 hours. When marinated, place in an oven at 180°C for 7 minutes, take out and allow to cool, then remove the string and freeze.

For the sorbet, blanch four yellow peppers in slightly salted water, deseed, peel off the skins and blend, finally passing the pulp through a fine sieve. Add 250g of the syrup made by boiling the caster sugar, glucose syrup and water until completely melted through, together with Galliano to taste. Place in an ice cream machine for 30-35 minutes, then store in the freezer until required.

To make the biscuits, melt the honey and butter in a saucepan, remove from the heat, sieve in the flour and add the egg whites. Mix thoroughly, then pipe the mix in swirled discs on a baking tray and bake at 170°C until golden brown.

To serve, thinly slice the frozen duck and arrange on the plate. Place a biscuit in the centre of the arrangement, topped with a ball of sorbet. Garnish each serving with two sprigs of chive.

Steamed corn fed chicken with red pimento mousse and honey braised leeks

Serves 4

Ingredients:

2 corn fed chickens

4 red peppers

2 egg yolks

100ml double cream

Herb brioche breadcrumbs

For the honey braised leeks:

2 large leeks

2 shallots

60g honey

30ml white wine

Carefully remove the leg and breast meat from the chickens. Place the carcass and bones in a pan and make a stock for the leeks by boiling with a little white wine and a mirepoix of vegetables.

Blanch the red peppers in slightly salted water until soft, remove the skins, and place in a blender with the leg meat. Blend together slowly, adding the egg yolks, cream, and salt and pepper until it becomes a mousse. Pass the mousse through a fine sieve into piping bag. Make an incision in the breasts to form a pocket – starting at the thick end and being careful not to pierce right through – and fill each with mousse. Wrap each filled breast in cling film in a cylindrical shape and leave in the fridge until needed.

Top and tail the leeks (but otherwise leave them whole), soak them in hot water for five minutes then rinse under cold water and place in a roasting dish. Dice the shallots and sweat them in a saucepan; add the white wine and reduce by half. Add the honey, chicken stock, salt and pepper and bring to the boil, then pour the liquid over the leeks until they are covered. Place in a hot oven (180°C) for 30-35 minutes.

Steam the chicken breasts for 15 minutes in their film, unwrap, roll in the herb brioche breadcrumbs then shallow fry until golden brown. To present, cut each of the braised leeks into six pieces and place three on each plate with a sliced chicken breast.

Pear mousse in a chocolate cup, Poire William sabayon

Serves 4

For the mousse:

150ml stock syrup

150ml pear purée

4 leaves gelatine

*450ml whipping cream
(semi whipped)*

30ml Poire William

2 poached pears

For the chocolate cup:

250g dark chocolate

For the Poire William sabayon:

4 egg yolks

125g caster sugar

30ml Poire William

Soak the gelatine in cold water and add to the heated stock syrup. Remove from the heat and add the pear purée and Poire William then place in the fridge until slightly setting. At this point fold in the semi whipped cream and return to the fridge to set.

For the chocolate cup, select plastic moulds of the required dimensions. Melt the chocolate over a bain marie and brush the melted chocolate onto the moulds. Leave to harden, then repeat the process twice. Once the third coating has set, turn out the moulds and keep the cups refrigerated until required. Use the remaining chocolate to make chocolate curls. To prepare the sabayon whisk the egg yolks, sugar, and Poire Wiliam over a ban marie until at the ribbon stage and white in colour.

To serve, slice the poached pears into strips and arrange around the plate. Spoon the sabayon over the pear strips and glaze. Pipe the mousse into the cups and place at the centre, decorated with chocolate curls and icing sugar if required.

PASTRY CHEF: DAVID SHIERS

THE PRIORY BAY HOTEL

Gary Moreton-Jones

Paella of seabass and scallops

Serves 4

Ingredients:

4 small fillets of seabass

4 scallops

75ml white wine

3 tablespoons olive oil

200g arborio risotto rice

1 teaspoon turmeric

450ml fish stock

500g fresh cockles

200g fresh mussels

50g Parmesan

150g butter

25g coriander, chopped

2 shallots, chopped

1 clove garlic, chopped

12 sprigs chervil, on ice

Heat up the fish stock; meanwhile sweat one of the shallots, add the rice and turmeric, and gently add the warmed fish stock until the rice is tender but still has bite. In a separate pan sweat the other shallot and the garlic, then add the cockles, mussels and wine and cover for three minutes. Take out half of the cooked seafood and put it aside to keep fresh in its shells: shell the remaining cockles and mussels and return the meat to the pan.

Heat two tablespoons of the oil in a non stick pan and cook the seasoned fillets for two minutes on the skin side and one minute turned. While the fish is cooking, stir half the butter, the Parmesan, the chopped coriander and the shelled seafood into the risotto: season to taste. In a non stick pan bring one tablespoon of olive oil to smoking and pan fry the scallops for a minute each side.

To serve shape the risotto on the plate with a ring, placing the fish on top. Scatter the seafood in its shells around the centre, place a scallop on each plate, drizzle with olive oil, and garnish with the chervil.

Guinea fowl with beurre noisette jus

Serves 4

Ingredients:

2 guinea fowl

1 chicken breast

100g duck foie gras

200g sliced pancetta

300g girolle mushrooms

4 baby carrots

4 baby turnips

100g trompette mushrooms

450g butter

400ml single cream

200g fresh peas

6 shallots

Juice of half a lemon

1 clove garlic

100g chopped parsley

100g chopped chives

450ml guinea fowl/chicken stock

1 egg white

4 medium potatoes

Remove and bone the legs of the guinea fowl, trim the crown of excess fat and skin, but keep the skin covering the breast. Loosen this, and first rub underneath with half the butter, then stuff the gap between meat and skin with half the chopped herbs and garlic.

Blend the chicken breast with half a teaspoon of salt in a blender, then add the egg white and the cream and continue blending until white. Transfer the mix to a bowl and add the rest of the herbs and the diced foie gras. Season the boned legs and lay each on a slice of pancetta with a tablespoon of the mousse, wrap the pancetta around to form a sausage shaped parcel, then tightly roll the parcel in cling film. Poach these in boiling water for 12 minutes. Cut the potatoes with a round cutter and cook them uncovered in 200g of the butter plus half the stock for 35-40 minutes, then set aside to keep warm.

Roast the crowns for 25 minutes on each side at 180°C; leave the meat to rest for eight minutes, then remove the breasts. Meanwhile, sauté two of the shallots and add the rest of the stock, reducing by two thirds. Cook the rest of the shallots, carrots, and turnips in a separate pan until tender, then glaze with butter and season. Set out the fondant potatoes on hot plates, topping each with the root vegetables.

Heat up two pans. Remove the cling film from the parcels and heat the poached legs in one until the pancetta is crisped, then take the pan off the heat and add the wild mushrooms and peas for one minute: plate with the roasted breasts. In the other pan, add the rest of the butter and, when frothy, add the lemon juice and the stock reduction. Spoon the sauce over the guinea fowl and serve.

Peach melba

Serves 4

Vanilla parfait:

450ml double cream

4 egg yolks

110g sugar

3 vanilla pods

Beat the egg yolks in a mixer until light and pale; whip the cream with the vanilla to soft peak. Boil the sugar with the water, then pour over the yolks and beat while the mixture cools. When it is cool, fold it into the cream and pour the parfait into moulds, then freeze for six hours.

Poached peaches:

4 peaches

1 vanilla pod

2 star anise

1 cinnamon stick

Zest of 1 orange & 1 lemon

500g sugar

500ml water

Peel the peaches. Mix together all the other ingredients in a pan, add the peaches, then bring to the boil and simmer for five minutes. Allow the peaches to cool in the syrup.

Florentine biscuit:

250g flaked almonds

50g double cream

110g sultanas

50g chopped peel

50g chopped pistachios

50g glacé cherries

175g sugar

175g butter

Gently caramelise the sugar and butter in a large pan. Mix in the fruit and nuts; when fully blended, add the cream. Take off the heat, stirring to continue integration, then spread the mix thinly over a baking sheet and bake for between 10 and 15 minutes at 150˚C.

Assemble as shown.

RIBER HALL

Michael Thompson

Seared scallops, tomato tian, and a cherry tomato essence

Serves 4

Ingredients:

12 scallops

For the tian:

8 plum tomatoes

2 shallots

2 cloves garlic

4 sprigs basil

Balsamic vinegar

Olive oil

50ml crème fraîche

1 large basil leaf

For the essence:

200g vine cherry tomatoes

12 sprigs basil

Prepare the essence by blitzing the tomatoes and basil with a little salt for ten seconds, then hanging the liquid to drain through muslin for two hours. Store in a cool place until needed.

For the tian, blanch the tomatoes in boiling water for 10-12 seconds and refresh with iced water, then peel, quarter and deseed. Prepare a marinade with the chopped shallots, garlic, a sprig of basil, balsamic vinegar, olive oil and salt. Marinate the tomato petals for four hours, then press in layers into four cylinder moulds and leave to set.

Prepare the basil crème fraîche by hanging the cream in muslin for two to three hours to drain off the watery liquid, then fold in the chopped basil leaf. Store in the fridge.

Pan fry the scallops for around a minute each side in very hot oil. Turn out a tian at 12 o'clock on each plate, then arrange three scallops at 6 o'clock. Pour the essence into the bowl to form a shallow pool at its base, and finish with a quenelle of crème fraîche garnished with a sprig of basil – plus caviar if desired – lightly placed on each tian.

Assiette of lamb with a Mediterranean vegetable tian

Serves 4

Ingredients:

4 x 75g fillet of lamb loin

300g lamb's kidneys

4 sheets caul fat 5 x 5cm

4 leaves coriander to garnish

For the pithiviers:

175g lamb shank

120g puff pastry

1200ml veal glaze

400ml chicken stock

For the tian:

2 courgettes, finely sliced

2 aubergines

1 each red, green, and yellow peppers

For the lentils:

2 shallots, finely diced

2 cloves of garlic, chopped

400g Puy lentils

4 sprigs rosemary

4 sprigs thyme

1200ml chicken stock

For the sauce:

400ml veal (or chicken) stock

2 sprigs rosemary

2 cloves garlic

For the cabbage:

1 small Savoy cabbage

2 slices Parma ham, diced

100g butter

For the fondant:

1 large swede

2 cloves garlic

400ml chicken stock

400g butter

2 sprigs thyme

1 bay leaf

Cut the aubergines into half inch slices, press out the bitter juice, then cook in olive oil until golden brown on both sides. Season the slices and set aside. Deseed and dice the peppers, then sauté in olive until tender. Slice the courgettes as finely as possible, ideally with a mandolin, then blanch in boiling salted water for twenty seconds and refresh in iced water. To create the tian, layer the vegetables – first aubergine, then peppers, aubergines again, finally courgettes – in circular moulds, fanning the final layer of courgettes on top of the tian.

To prepare the pithiviers, braise the lamb shank in the stocks for a good three hours at 150°C, until the meat falls off the bone. Separate and season the meat. Roll out the puff pastry to a thickness of around 3mm, then cut out eight 5cm discs. Divide the shank meat into four, placing a portion in the centre of four of the discs, then cover each with a second disc and 'ravioli' by firmly sealing the edges; use egg wash to be extra careful, although water should be sufficient. Cook in the oven at 150°C for 12-15 minutes.

For the rest of the assiette, divide the kidneys into four and roll the whole kidneys into a sheet of caul, tying in three places along the length of the cylindrical parcel. Wrap the parcels tightly in cling film and leave them in the fridge for a couple of hours to set. Remove the cling film and sear with oil on all sides over a moderate heat in a frying pan, then cook for no more than three minutes in a hot oven (180°C); rest for two minutes before serving. Seal, cook, and rest the loins in the same way.

Peel the swede and divide into four, then cut out four cylinders with a round cutter – bear this in mind when buying your swede. Braise the fondants in the stock for around 45 minutes until tender. Braise the lentils with the chopped shallot, garlic, and herbs in the stock for around 30 minutes at the same temperature until they are tender. Set both aside to keep warm. Remove all the outer leaves from the cabbage and cut out the stalk, leaving just the tender inner leaves. Finely chop, then sweat with the Parma ham in foaming butter: keep this warm also. Meanwhile, reduce the veal stock with the chopped garlic and rosemary to a good sauce consistency, then strain and keep warm.

Reheat the tians either in the oven or the microwave. If the latter, about 90 seconds at full power should be enough (check by inserting a knife into the centre of one; if it is warm on the lip, the tian is ready). Meanwhile, prepare the plate with a ring of cabbage surmounted by lentils, with the sliced loin on top. Slice the kidney parcels, and arrange with the pithiviers, the swede and the tian. Drizzle around the sauce, and garnish the loin with coriander and the tian with basil.

Raspberry millefeuille with mandarin sorbet

Serves 4

Ingredients:

3 punnets raspberries

Mint leaves for garnish

For the coconut tuile:

150g icing sugar

100g egg white

100g desiccated coconut

85g butter

For the praline cream:

300ml double cream

1/2 tablespoon icing sugar

2 drops vanilla essence

30g fresh praline

For the raspberry coulis:

100g raspberries

Juice of half a lemon

1 tablespoon caster sugar

For the mandarin sorbet:

400ml mandarin purée

100g caster sugar

Melt the butter for the coconut tuiles, then pour the melted butter over the other ingredients in a bowl, stirring until fully blended. Once cooled, leave in the fridge to set, then spread the mix thinly over non-stick paper or mat on a baking tray. Make a template to cut out triangles: 12 tuiles will be needed. Bake at 100°C for around ten minutes until golden brown, then leave to cool and harden.

Whisk together the ingredients for the praline cream to a stiff peak, then fill a piping bag with the mix and set aside. For the coulis, boil half the caster sugar with a little water until the sugar dissolves to make a stock syrup. Blend the raspberries with the lemon juice and the remaining sugar until the mix is smooth, then pass through a fine sieve, using the stock syrup to adjust the consistency.

Prepare the sorbet by processing peeled mandarins until there is 400ml of fruit purée. Bring the purée and the sugar to the boil over a moderate heat, simmering until all the sugar has dissolved, then leave to cool. Churn in a machine, then freeze.

To assemble the dish, arrange raspberries along the sides of a tuile and pipe praline cream to fill the centre. Cover the tuile with another and repeat the process, dusting the 'roof' with icing sugar and garnishing with three raspberries and a sprig of mint. Place a quenelle of praline cream and a ball of sorbet alongside the millefeuille: dot coulis across the plate for a final flourish.

THE ROMAN CAMP

Ian McNaught

Poached lobster with basil custard

Serves 4

Ingredients:

*2 lobsters, cooked and shelled
(keep the shells)*

28 slices of small cucumber

2 tablespoons chives, finely chopped

*2 tablespoons black olives,
finely chopped*

4 tablespoons pesto

*4 plum tomatoes,
skinned, deseeded, and diced*

4 teaspoons Avruga caviar

4 basil leaves, deep fried

For the lobster broth:

Lobster shells

2 tablespoons olive oil

*100g each:
leek, shallot, celery, and tomato*

75ml cognac

1 clove garlic, chopped

Small pinch saffron thread

200ml fish stock

200ml shellfish stock

Small bunch basil

2 fillets lemon sole

4 egg whites

For the basil custard:

180ml milk

180ml double cream

3 eggs

2 tablespoons fresh basil purée

Begin the lobster broth by heating the oil in a pan and frying off the lobster shells, then add the vegetables and cook until they are lightly coloured. Deglaze the pan with the cognac and add the garlic and saffron. Finally add the stocks and basil and bring the pan to the boil.

Simmer for between 45 minutes and an hour, then pass the liquid through muslin into a clean pan and allow to cool slightly. Meanwhile liquidise the sole fillets and egg whites and add these to the broth; place the pan over a low heat and cook gently until the egg white has set and the stock is clear. Pass through muslin again, adjust the seasoning, and chill until required.

To prepare the basil custard bring the milk to the boil with the cream, then add the eggs and whisk away from the heat until the mix is cool. Add the basil purée and pass through a sieve; check the seasoning, then pour into moulds. Cook in a foil-covered bain marie at 150°C for 20-30 minutes: the custards are ready when they are firm to the touch. Leave to cool, then chill until needed.

When ready, turn out the custards, topping each with caviar and a deep fried basil leaf. Mix together the tomatoes, olives, chives, cucumber, and pesto, and arrange in a ring around the bowl or plate. Divide up and season the lobster – half a tail sliced and a claw per person – and gently pour the chilled broth around the dish.

Loué chicken and foie gras ballotine, truffle gnocchi, fumet of cep

Serves 4

For the ballotine:

4 Loué chicken breasts

4 strips foie gras

100g chicken mousseline

4 slices Parma ham

For the gnocchi:

250g dry mashed potatoes

100g plain flour

1 egg yolk

50g chopped truffle

1 teaspoon truffle essence

For the cep fumet:

2 teaspoons olive oil

50g each finely chopped carrot, leek, onion and celery

60g dried ceps

Trimmings from wild mushrooms

1 sprig thyme

50ml port

50ml Madeira

1 chicken leg

250ml veal stock

250ml chicken stock

100ml water

To accompany:

400g spinach

12 small carrots, cooked

12 asparagus tips, cooked

200g wild mushrooms

60g butter

To prepare the ballotines, remove the skin from the breasts, then make two incisions outwards from the centre of each so that they spread out to make one flat piece. Season the meat, cover it with an even layer of the mousseline, then lay a strip of foie gras along the middle and roll up into a sausage shape. Wrap this roll firstly in Parma ham, then tightly into cling film: finally, seal each ballotine with foil and chill until required.

For the gnocchi, gently mix together and season all the ingredients, then on a floured surface roll the mix into balls – allow five per serving. Cook the balls in boiling salted water for five minutes, then drain, toss in a little oil, and chill until needed.

Heat the oil in a saucepan. Cook the vegetables for the fumet until brown, then add the dried ceps, the mushroom trimmings, and the thyme. Deglaze the pan with the port and Madeira, then add the chicken leg, veal, stocks, and water. Bring the pan to the boil, skimming as required, then simmer for one and a half hours. Pass the liquid through muslin into a clean pan and reduce over a high heat until a good sauce consistency is reached.

When ready to serve, poach the ballotines in the cling film in boiling water for 12 minutes, then rest for three to four minutes. Meanwhile cook the mushrooms and spinach in 40g of the butter, and reheat the gnocchi, carrots, and asparagus in the remaining butter with two tablespoons of water. Reheat the cep fumet. Unwrap and slice the ballotines; place the spinach in the centre of the plate under the slices with the vegetables and gnocchi arranged about, and pour the fumet moderately around the plate.

Passion fruit jelly with coconut sorbet, pineapple fritters

Serves 4

For the jelly:

10 passion fruit

Juice of 2 oranges

3 leaves gelatine

100g sugar

100ml water

12 raspberries

4 sprigs mint

Soak the gelatine in cold water; meanwhile, scoop out the passion fruit and add the flesh to the orange juice, sugar, and water in a pan. Bring the pan to the boil, then take off the heat and skim off the surface. Add the gelatine to dissolve, then pass the liquid first through a fine sieve, then through muslin. Pour into glasses and chill until set.

For the coconut sorbet:

500ml coconut purée

50ml Malibu

50g liquid glucose

200g caster sugar

400ml water

4 brandy snap baskets

Bring the sugar, water, and glucose to the boil, simmer for 10 minutes, and remove from the heat. Allow to cool, then whisk in the coconut purée and Malibu. Churn in an ice cream machine and freeze until needed.

For the pineapple fritters:

12 chunks of fresh pineapple

100g self raising flour

10ml dark rum

160ml soda water

Sugar for dusting

Sieve the flour into a bowl, then whisk in the rum and soda water to make a smooth batter. Dip the pineapple into the batter and deep fry at 180°C until golden and crisp.

To serve, top the jelly with three raspberries and a sprig of mint. Place three pineapple fritters on each plate and scoop the sorbet into brandy snap baskets: shown here with a tuile cigarette topping the sorbet.

SEAHAM HALL HOTEL & ORIENTAL SPA
John Connell

Scottish langoustines with sweet spices and a light fennel bavarois

Serves 4

Ingredients:

16 large langoustines

1 teaspoon dried orange powder (method below)

Juice from 2 large heads of fennel (approximately 30ml)

100ml double cream

100ml fresh orange juice

1g fennel pollen

1/4 teaspoon spice mix (orange powder, cinnamon, coriander, star anise)

1 1/2 leaves gelatine (bronze)

8 pieces baby fennel for garnish

100ml shellfish bisque

To make the orange powder lay out the shredded peel of 10 oranges on a tray, ensuring as little pith as possible remains, and leave for 24 hours in a 60°C oven to dry. When ready, the dried peel should crumble in the fingers. Finely blitz the dried peels, grinding until superfine, then pass through a very fine sieve. The result will be two tablespoons of intensely flavoured and coloured orange 'pollen'. Use the same method with the residue from the juiced fennel for the fennel pollen.

Melt the gelatine in 60ml of fennel juice, then combine with the rest of the fennel juice, the fennel pollen, and the cream. Season to taste, then pour into ring moulds lined with cling film and place in the fridge for four to six hours.

Blanch the langoustines for 30 seconds in salted boiling water, then lightly sauté over a medium heat; take off the heat and add spice mix and orange powder while still warm to infuse with flavour. Add the orange juice and reduce the liquid to half glaze, then remove from the heat and sprinkle with a little more of the orange powder and spices to taste.

To serve, remove the claws and arrange four langoustines on one side of the plate, a little of the glaze poured over each, with one of the bavarois turned out alongside them. Crack the claws and garnish the bavarois with the meat. Decorate the plate with baby fennel, orange powder, crisped hearts of fennel – microwave at full power under cling film on a plate for one minute, then leave out to dry – and shellfish bisque foamed with a hand blender and spooned on or applied with a foam gun.

Asian roasted seafood

Serves 4

Some of these ingredients – the pandan (a SE Asian flax) and banana leaves and the galangal – may only be obtainable from specialist Asian shops. These are fascinating places full of unusual and exciting foodstuff like the ginger salt and pickled beansprouts recommended to be served with this dish.

Ingredients:

4 extra large diver scallops

4 medallions tuna, sashami grade

4 large pieces of lobster (claw or tail)

8 pieces sprouting broccoli

6 sticks lemon grass

1cm galangal ginger

250g butter

50g mustard oil

*150g Thai jasmine
or royal jasmine rice*

300ml coconut milk

1 pandan leaf

1 large young banana leaf

2 red peppers

Icing sugar

Prepare an aromatic butter by extracting the central leaves around 2cm from the foot of the cut stalk from the lemon grass and chopping them to an ultrafine dice. Grind the galangal to the same consistency: combine both with the butter, then blend to a smooth paste and pass through a fine sieve.

Cook the rice in the coconut milk with the aromatic pandan leaf. Cut out four large discs from the most pliable section of the banana leaf; when the rice is ready, take out the Pandan and divide the rice onto the four discs. Roll each into a parcel, seal with toothpicks or similar, and set aside.

For the pepper tuiles, roast two red peppers until the skin is blistered. Take off the skin and remove the seeds, then weigh the flesh: add half this weight in icing sugar and blitz the 2:1 pepper/sugar mix to a smooth paste in a blender. Shape the tuiles on a non stick baking mat with the fingers, leave to harden, then bake for ten minutes at 150°C. Remove from the oven and while still warm peel them from the mat and press one side against a cold surface,

for example the inside of the fridge. This gives a pleasing shine to the pressed side. Store in an airtight container with silica gel if they are not being used immediately.

Next sauté the seafood lightly in the mustard oil, and when cooked – make sure that the tuna, which should be rare, does not overcook – add 50g of the aromatic butter. When foaming, add the sprouting broccoli. Set aside.

Steam the rice parcels for twelve minutes and put one on each plate. Arrange the seafood, garnishing with broccoli and a small pool of lemon grass and galangal butter for dipping. Finally, place a pepper tuile on top of the seafood.

SHARROW BAY

Juan Martin/Colin Akrigg

Pan-fried scallops on roasted asparagus with chive butter sauce

Serves 4

Ingredients:

16 asparagus spears

12 scallops

For the chive butter sauce:

1 tablespoon white wine vinegar

2 tablespoons white wine

1 tablespoon butter

1 tablespoon double cream

1 teaspoon chopped chives

1 dessertspoon finely diced shallots

4oz unsalted butter

8 whole chives for garnish

Olive oil

Place the tablespoon of butter and the shallots into a heavy based saucepan and heat until the shallots are translucent, then add the white wine vinegar. Reduce this by half, then add the white wine; continue reducing until a syrupy consistency is achieved. To this reduction add the double cream and whisk in the unsalted butter until it has been completely absorbed and the mixture is creamy. Once this texture is reached remove from the heat and pass through a fine chinois into a clean pan. Season and add the finely chopped chives just before serving.

For the asparagus, firstly trim the spears to even lengths, lightly peeling the stalky ends. Coat them in a little olive oil and lightly season, then place under a medium grill for two minutes. Turn each spear and cook for a further two minutes: set aside to keep warm.

Prepare fresh scallops by removing them from the shell and washing them thoroughly: for this dish the white flesh only is required and the roe can be discarded. Once prepared, lightly season the scallops and brown them in a hot sauté pan in a little olive oil for about one minute each side.

To serve, place four roasted asparagus spears on each plate, on which sit three scallops. Arrange two whole chives on the scallops for garnish, finally drizzle the warm chive butter sauce around the asparagus.

Roast quail on fondant potato with wild mushroom and Madeira sauce

Serves 4

Ingredients:

4 quail

4 potatoes

100g spinach

24 wild mushrooms for garnish

For the sauce:

3 shallots, sliced

4 mushrooms, sliced

1 clove of garlic, crushed

1 sprig of thyme

1 bay leaf

115ml Madeira

75g unsalted butter

575ml brown chicken stock

2 tablespoons of demi glaze (optional)

To prepare the Madeira sauce, sweat the shallots, mushrooms, garlic, thyme, and bay leaf in one third of the butter. After a few minutes, when a lighter colour emerges, add the Madeira and reduce the liquid by two thirds. Add the chicken stock and reduce by two thirds again. Finally, whisk in the remaining butter to create a glazed consistency, then pass through a fine chinois into a clean pan.

For the fondant potatoes, first select potatoes large enough to be cut into rectangles roughly 2" wide by 1" deep. Reshape these rectangles into oval shapes by paring away the corners. Place butter in a 6" non stick oven proof pan, add the potato ovals, cover with water, and bring to a simmer. Cover the pan with buttered parchment and place in a preheated oven at 200°C until the potato is cooked (about twenty minutes). Return the pan to the hot plate and bring it to a rapid boil, continuing until all the liquor has evaporated and the potato is a light golden brown.

To prepare the buttered spinach, select fresh crisp leaves and wash copiously in clean water. Place in a pan with a little butter, season with salt, and cook for a few moments until the leaves are soft. Remove from the heat and keep warm. For the mushroom garnish, select for shape, trim and wash 24 wild mushrooms. Lightly cook them in a sauté pan with a little butter and a tablespoon of water until tender, then remove from the heat and keep warm.

The four quail should be evenly sized young birds. Heat a little oil in a medium sized sauté pan, then seal each bird until it is a light golden brown all over. Place the quail in a preheated oven at 220°C for five minutes, then allow to rest in a warm place for a further five minutes. Immediately prior to serving remove the legs and the breasts from the bone.

To serve the dish place the warm spinach in the centre of the plate with the fondant on top, arranging the quail on top of the potato. Garnish with mushrooms and place the whole dish under a preheated grill for a few seconds, then drizzle with the Madeira sauce.

Dark chocolate parfait encased in a caramel box with a raspberry sauce

6 portions

For the caramel box:

575g caster sugar

2 teaspoons glucose

4 tablespoons ground almonds

Boil the sugar and glucose with a little water until it is a golden colour, then pour the liquid onto silicon paper and allow to cool and set. When hard, break it up into small chunks and blitz in a blender with the ground almonds to form a powder. Spread this to a depth of 2mm in a baking tray lined with silicon paper, place in the oven and allow to melt. Remove and cut while soft into the desired shape and size with an oiled knife; allow to set hard. Store in an airtight container.

To make the box, lightly seal the edges with liquid caramel and leave to set. Fill with the parfait, topping with whatever berries are in season.

For the dark chocolate parfait:

220g egg yolk

400g caster sugar

1 litre double cream

300g dark chocolate

Set the egg yolks to whisk in a processor while the sugar boils with a little water to hard ball (121°C); pour the sugar over the egg yolks and continue to whisk until the mix is cold. Melt the chocolate over a bain marie and allow to cool. Semi whip the cream, then mix together all the ingredients and pipe into moulds. Place in the freezer until frozen.

To make the sugar springs, heat together sugar and glucose in a pan with a little water: when this caramel mix has thickened, slowly but regularly drizzle from a spoon in one hand onto a metal pole being gently rotated in the other (practice makes perfect). Leave to set, then carefully prise off.

For the raspberry sauce:

100g fresh raspberries

10g icing sugar

Blitz together the ingredients, then finely sieve the liquid and keep cool.

SHEEN FALLS LODGE
Chris Farrell

Ravioli of caramelised Autumn root vegetables, plum tomato fondue, cappucino of bay leaf

Serves 4

For the pasta:

500g strong flour

1 whole egg

1 egg yolk

200ml water

For the tomato fondue:

1 shallot, diced

1 teaspoon tomato purée

150ml Noilly Prat

4 plum tomato, concassé

1 sprig rosemary

For the ravioli filling:

200g mirepoix of carrot, celeriac, celery, parsnip, shallot

1/2 teaspoon chopped rosemary

1/2 teaspoon chopped herbs (eg chives & flat parsley)

1 teaspoon sugar

For the cappucino:

50g mirepoix onion, leek, celery

25g butter

1 teaspoon sherry vinegar

200ml stock (chicken or vegetable)

4 bay leaves

200ml double cream

Sweat off the vegetables for the ravioli filling in the caramelised sugar. Take off the heat, season, and when cool add the herbs. Meanwhile, combine the ingredients for the pasta in a blender until they make a firm ball of dough. Roll out the dough in a machine or as thinly as possible with a rolling pin. Cut out four discs of around 7cm across and four of twice the diameter: divide the vegetables into four, place a mound on each of the small discs, then drape a large disc over the top. Press in the pasta to prevent air bubbles and make sure the discs are firmly sealed together, then chill the ravioli for at least 30 minutes.

For the bay leaf cappucino, sweat the vegetables in the butter then deglaze with the sherry vinegar. Add the stock, bay leaves, and cream, and cook lightly for 35 minutes, then strain and leave to one side.

To prepare the fondue, sweat off the shallots with the purée and rosemary, then deglaze with the Noilly Prat. Add the tomatoes and cook lightly: season to taste.

Reheat the sauce and the fondue in separate pans while cooking the ravioli in seasoned boiling water for four minutes. Place the fondue in a soup plate with the ravioli above: whirl the bay leaf sauce to a frothy finish with a hand blender and serve as shown.

Roast saddle of venison with braised cos, celeriac, baby leek, and bitter chocolate sauce

Serves 4

Ingredients:

4 x 200g fillets wild venison loin

4 potatoes, peeled and eyed

2 heads baby cos, sliced

1 rasher smoked streaky bacon, chopped

8 baby leeks

*300ml veal jus
(convenience gravy will substitute)*

*100g bitter chocolate drops
(72% cocoa content)*

10g celeriac, cut into 20 large pieces

Clarified butter

Butter

Sugar

3 shallots

1 teaspoon tarragon vinegar

200ml Noilly Prat

200ml chicken stock

300ml single cream

1/2 clove of garlic (optional)

Check the pieces of meat and remove any sinew or gristle, then season the fillets with freshly milled pepper and leave to one side. Blanch and refresh the celeriac and baby leeks. Individually grate the potatoes and cook each in clarified butter in a hot small sauté or blinis pan, taking care to brown the potato 'pancake' evenly on both sides.

Seal the venison with a little oil on a hot pan, then cook either in the oven at 180°C or under the grill to the required degree. At the same time sweat off the baby cos with a little butter and the bacon; taste and season. Lightly heat the veal jus and melt in the chocolate drops, being careful not to let the sauce boil or it may curdle.

To prepare a shallot cream for the vegetables, sweat off the peeled and sliced shallots (with the chopped garlic if preferred) in a little butter with a pinch of sugar, then deglaze with the tarragon vinegar. Add the Noilly Prat and reduce by a third, then add the chicken stock and reduce by a third again. Stir in the cream and simmer for five minutes, then pass through a sieve and adjust the seasoning.

Allow the meat to rest before carving. Sweat off the baby leeks with a little butter, and caramelise the celeriac. Place the baby cos in the centre of the plate with the potato rösti above, with carved slices of venison on top. Arrange the celeriac and leeks around the plate: reheat the shallot cream and buzz with a hand blender to foam, then drizzle the cream over the vegetables and pour the chocolate sauce over the meat.

Chocolate tuile barrel with marinated cherries and fromage blanc mousse

Serves 4

Marinated black cherries:

100g black cherries

100ml red wine

1 cinnamon stick

1 star anise

1 vanilla pod

50ml raspberry coulis

50g sugar

Stone the cherries. Melt the other ingredients in a pan then lightly poach the cherries in the syrup for around 15 minutes. Strain and set aside to cool. A reduction of the syrup will provide a garnish for the dish.

Chocolate tuile:

75g butter

60g egg white

75g sugar

50g strong flour

100g cocoa powder

25g chopped pistachios

Cream the butter and sugar with the paddle in a blender. Add half the egg white, flour, and the sieved cocoa powder and continue to blend; once all the ingredients have combined, blend in the rest of the egg white. Leave the mix to cool for at least three hours, then roll it out thinly in 8cm square on a baking tray, spreading the pistachios in a band across the centre of each square. Use any mix left over for additional tuiles for decoration. Bake at 170°C for three minutes, then wrap the squares around a rolling pin or appropriately sized cylinder to harden into barrel shapes. Keep dry while storing.

Pistachio macaronade:

100g ground almonds

20g cream flour

100g egg white

100g sugar

1 teaspoon pistachio paste

Mix together the almonds, flour, and half the sugar. Whisk the egg whites with the rest of the sugar until white and stiffened; use a little of the meringue to blend with the pistachio paste into a cream. Fold the dry mixture into the meringue, and blend in the pistachio cream. Pipe the mixture into macaroon shapes on a baking tray and bake for 15 minutes at 170°C.

Fromage blanc mousse:

20ml water

60g sugar

1 egg

1 leaf gelatine (soaked in cold water)

1 egg yolk

200g fromage blanc (0% fat)

250ml whipped cream

Bring the sugar and water to 120°C, then whisk the eggs and beat the sugar syrup into the eggs until the mix is cold. In a separate pan, dissolve the gelatine into a little of the fromage blanc over a low heat. Fold first the cream, then the gelatine, and finally the rest of the fromage blanc, into the egg mixture, continue stirring until cold, then set aside.

Kirsch sabayon:

3 egg yolks

50g sugar

50ml kirsch

50ml whipped cream

Whisk the egg yolks, sugar and kirsch over a bain marie to 80°C, then continue whisking until the mix is cold. Fold in the whipped cream, then pour into flat rings of around 8cm and store in the fridge until required.

To assemble the dish, arrange a disc of the sabayon in the centre of each plate with a chocolate barrel on top. Insert the pistachio macaronade and chopped marinated cherries into the barrel, with the fromage blanc mousse completing the filling. Shown here garnished with chocolate tuiles, the reduced red wine syrup, and candied pistachios.

Luke Tipping

Tronçonnettes of lobster, truffled spaghettini, lobster & pepper sauce

Serves 4

Ingredients:

2 x 700g native lobsters

400g cooked spaghettini

10g truffle, chopped

For the sauce:

2 lobster heads

7 plum tomatoes, chopped

2 red peppers, deseeded and chopped

1 shallot

100g Parma ham, sliced

500ml chicken stock

200ml double cream

Kill the lobsters by inserting the point of a heavy knife between the eyes. Remove the claws and tail, then chop off the heads and reserve for the sauce. Blanch the claws for two minutes and the tail for thirty seconds in heavily salted boiling water, then refresh in iced water. Crack the claws with a small hammer and remove the meat, and divide the tails into four pieces each along the natural lines of the shell. Boil the spaghettini and set aside in cold water.

To prepare the sauce, chop the lobster heads and fry them in olive oil until they turn pink. Add the shallot, tomatoes, peppers and Parma ham, and cook until soft. Cover with the chicken stock and bring to the boil, then reduce the heat and simmer for one hour. Pass the liquid through a strainer into a clean pan, then return to the boil. Add the double cream, cook for two minutes on a reduced heat, then keep warm.

Season the lobster meat with rock salt and olive oil, then place under a hot grill until cooked (about two minutes). Reheat the spaghettini in butter and olive oil, adding the chopped truffle and salt and white pepper to season. To serve, fork a generous twist of spaghettini onto each plate, together with two pieces of tail and one claw. Foam the sauce with a hand blender and spoon over the meat.

Honey glazed shank of lamb, aubergine caviar, lemon couscous with its own juice

Serves 4

Ingredients:

4 shanks of lamb

500g root vegetables, chopped

50g saffron

100ml Madeira

500ml chicken stock

3 plum tomatoes

3 cloves of garlic

2 aubergines

200g couscous

1 tablespoon sultanas

2 spring onions, chopped

1 bunch flat leaf parsley

Juice of 1 lemon

20g cumin seeds

20g pumpkin seeds

Olive oil

100g butter

1 tablespoon clear honey

In a deep pan, arrange the shanks with the bones pointing up and add the root vegetables (carrot, onion, celery), garlic, saffron, Madeira, tomatoes and cumin seeds. Pour in the chicken stock and bring to the boil. Skim, then cover and simmer on a low heat for three hours until the meat is tender. Leave to cool completely in the stock, preferably overnight. When cooled, the stock will form a jelly. Carefully extract the shanks, scraping back into the pan any jelly that clings, and boil the stock then strain to remove any solids: reserve and keep warm.

For the aubergine caviar, split the aubergines lengthwise and score the inners with a sharp knife. Season with olive oil and salt and pepper and wrap in foil, then bake for one hour at 180°C. Leave the aubergines to cool, then remove them from the foil and scrape out the insides with a spoon into a small pan. Cook the flesh on a low heat to remove any moisture until it becomes a smooth purée, then keep warm.

To prepare the lemon couscous, cover the sultanas with water in a saucepan and bring to the boil, then drain and pat them dry. Put the couscous into a large bowl and pour over just enough boiling water to be absorbed: add a little olive oil and fluff with a fork. Add the sultanas, pumpkin seeds, spring onions, finely chopped parsley, lemon juice, and salt to taste.

Place the lamb shanks on a roasting tray with 50g of the butter, and roast for thirty minutes at 220°C, basting so they are caramelised all over: season with salt and pepper, and spoon the honey over the meat. Arrange the couscous on four warm plates alongside a quenelle of aubergine caviar, placing the lamb shanks on top. Check the seasoning of the sauce, then whisk in the rest of the butter cut into cubes. When the sauce has thickened, pour over and serve immediately.

Dome of strawberries in champagne jelly with cheese ice cream

Serves 4

Ingredients:

500g strawberries

6 leaves gelatine

100ml cranberry juice

200g sugar

400ml pink champagne

For the ice cream:

375ml milk

3 egg yolks

300g cream cheese

375ml double cream

125g sugar

30g Roquefort cheese

For the tuiles:

150g butter

50g glucose

20g sesame seeds

150g caster sugar

50ml milk

50g poppy seeds

Soften the gelatine in cold water and squeeze dry. Meanwhile, bring the cranberry juice and sugar to the boil, whisk in the gelatine and champagne, then leave to cool.

Wash the strawberries if necessary and remove the stalks: if they are very large cut them into quarters, otherwise leave whole. Make sure the strawberries are dry. Line the bottom of four dome shaped moulds or bowls with the jelly mixture and leave to set. When set, add a layer of strawberries and cover with jelly: leave to set and repeat until the dome is full, but finish with a final layer of jelly only. Place in the fridge to set overnight.

For the ice cream, bring the cream and milk to the boil and take off the heat. Beat the sugar and yolks until they are thick and creamy, then pour the milk into the yolk mix, whisking continuously. Return the combined mix to a saucepan and add the cheeses, stirring with a spatula over a low heat until it thickens. Chill briefly, then churn in an ice cream machine until frozen.

To prepare sesame and poppy tuiles, stir the butter, sugar, glucose and milk over a low heat until they are melted together, then fold in the sesame and poppy seeds and leave to cool. Spread the mixture thinly on a non stick baking sheet and cook for about six minutes at 200°C until they are golden in colour. Take the sheet out of the oven and while it is still warm cut out discs the same diameter as the domes: leave to cool. To turn out the domes onto plates, dip the moulds briefly in hot water to loosen the jelly.

Simon Crannage

Hot sphere of goat's cheese, red onion and port purée

Serves 4

Ingredients:

500g good goat's cheese log

100g sunblush tomatoes, chopped

4 spring onions, chopped

3 red onions, chopped

4 shallots, chopped

2 eggs

140g plain flour

2 large baking potatoes, grated

500ml port

Heat the chopped red onions in a heavy pan with the port until the mixture is soft and dry, then blend on full speed until smooth.

Crumble the goat's cheese and, in a mixing bowl, blend with the chopped tomato, spring onion and shallots. When the ingredients are completely integrated, divide the mix into four equal portions and shape into balls. Mix together the flour and eggs and coat each ball with the mixture, then cover with grated potato, pressing to ensure a secure covering.

Deep fry the balls at 160°C until they are crisp and golden. Spread the onion purée over the centre of each plate with a cheese sphere in the centre. Serve with chutney and a simple green leaf salad.

Seared beef pavé, braised blade and horseradish faggot, red wine glaze

Serves 4

Ingredients:

4 x 150g beef rump steaks, thick cut

A half feather blade of beef

Casserole vegetables:
1 large carrot, 1 onion, 2 sticks celery

220g pork mince

110g horseradish root, grated

4 large spinach leaves

2 large baking potatoes

250ml good beef stock

2 large carrots, cut into batons

125ml red wine

Half a Savoy cabbage

Chervil and Maldon sea salt to garnish

To prepare the beef blade, preheat the oven to 120°C and place the blade in a casserole on top of the roughly chopped root vegetables. Add cold water to a depth of about 4cm, cover with foil and place in the oven until the meat is soft, usually about three and a half hours. Leave the blade to cool in the liquor: when cool, divide it into four equal pieces and put the meat back in the cooking liquid.

For the horseradish faggot, mix together the pork mince and horseradish in a mixing bowl and season with salt and pepper. Form four balls of equal size, and wrap each one in a blanched spinach leaf. Place the wrapped faggots in a heavy pan with half the beef stock and sufficient water to cover and simmer until tender to the touch, then set aside until needed.

Using a tall fondant cutter, cut four tall cylinders out of the potatoes and cook until tender in a pan with a good knob of butter and water to cover. Blanch and refresh the carrot and cabbage; then set the vegetables aside. Prepare the sauce by reducing the red wine by half and adding the beef stock, then reducing further until a good sauce consistency is achieved.

To serve, pan fry the rump steaks until medium and slice each into thin strips. Arrange the three vegetable garnishes in a line on the plate, then place the sliced steak on the cabbage, the blade on the carrots, and the faggot on the potato. Reheat the sauce and drizzle over the faggot and around the other components. Garnish with chervil and a few grains of Maldon sea salt.

Dark chocolate and banana fondant, rum ice with Malibu jelly

Serves 4

Fondant:

5 whole eggs

5 egg yolks

120g caster sugar

2 bananas, puréed

250g unsalted butter

10g plain four

250g bitter dark chocolate

Gently melt the chocolate and butter over hot water. Whisk the eggs, yolks, and sugar into a stiff sabayon consistency, then fold first the chocolate, then the flour and bananas, into the sabayon with a metal spoon. Refrigerate in a suitable container for three to four hours.

Butter and flour four dariole moulds, then fill each two thirds full and cook at 180°C until quite soft in the middle: this usually takes eight to ten minutes. Remove and leave to rest for one minute before turning out.

Rum ice:

6 egg yolks

140g caster sugar

250ml double cream

50ml navy rum

Juice of 1 lemon

250ml milk

Whisk the yolks and sugar until pale then add the rum and lemon juice. Bring the milk and cream to the boil in a thick bottomed pan, add a little to the yolk mixture to lessen the thickness, then add the yolk mixture to the milk and cream, stirring continuously over a low heat. When the liquid evenly coats the back of a spoon, strain it into a bowl and refrigerate: once cold, churn for 20 – 30 minutes, then freeze ready for use.

Banana crisp:

Preheat the oven to 130°C, then cut one firm banana lengthways into strips of around 2.5mm thickness each. Place the strips on silicone and cook for around 20 minutes until golden, then leave to cool. Store in an airtight container.

Malibu jelly:

100ml Malibu

100ml water

25g caster sugar

2 gelatine leaves (gold)

Soak the gelatine: heat the other ingredients in a pan until the sugar has dissolved, then add the gelatine and pass into a bowl, then place in the fridge to chill. When cooled but not firm, pour into the moulds over the set cream and return to the fridge to set.

Set cream:

250ml double cream

1 gelatine leaf (gold)

Juice of half a lemon

110g caster sugar

Quarter of a vanilla pod

Soak the gelatine in cold water while bringing all the other ingredients to the boil for one minute, then removing from the heat. Add the gelatine, then pour the mixture to a depth of around 5mm into small dariole moulds. Refrigerate to set.

To assemble, decorate the plate with lines of dotted caramel and chocolate sauce, then arrange with the fondant at the head and the jelly at the foot, with the ice and banana crisp at three o'clock. A sauce of mint is the perfect accompaniment to the Malibu jelly.

THE SWAN HOTEL

Shaun Naen

Glazed asparagus with sauce Maltaise

Serves 4

Ingredients:

*4 x 300g fresh asparagus,
peeled and trimmed*

50g shallots, chopped

50ml white wine vinegar

10 peppercorns, crushed

50ml cold water

6 egg yolks

600g clarified butter

70ml orange juice

Zest of one orange, blanched

For the sauce, reduce the vinegar, shallots and pepper in a saucepan until almost dry. Meanwhile place the cold water and egg yolks in a round bottom stainless steel bowl and whisk them together over a bain marie until the mixture gains the consistency of mayonnaise. Slowly pour in the clarified butter, stirring constantly, then add the seasoning, orange juice and zest. Finally, pass the reduced vinegar mixture through a chinois and add to the egg based mixture; beat in well, then keep at a moderate temperature until needed.

Add a pinch of salt to a large saucepan filled with water and bring to the boil. Add a knob of butter and the asparagus, then blanch for about five minutes until the spears are tender but still crunchy. Remove the asparagus and plunge it directly into iced water to prevent cooking further.

This dish can be served either hot or cold.

Slow cooked veal belly

Serves 4

Ingredients:

1kg boneless veal belly

200ml red wine

4 carrots, peeled and diced

*1 medium sized onion,
peeled and diced*

5 cloves garlic, crushed with skin on

1 celery stick, washed and diced

1 leek, washed and diced

250ml tomato juice

*250ml veal stock
(or chicken if unavailable)*

1 bouquet garni

6-7 tablespoons olive oil

Trim off any excess fat, then roll the belly along its length and tie into a sausage-shaped bundle. Season with salt and pepper, heat the olive oil in a heavy roasting tray and sear all sides until golden brown, then remove the meat to a casserole pot. Add the diced vegetables to the roasting tray and sauté until they begin to caramelise. Add the red wine and bring to the boil until all the alcohol has evaporated; finally pour in the tomato juice and stock and simmer for two to three minutes.

Pour the liquid into the casserole pot, augmenting with water if required to cover the meat. Bring the dish to a simmer on the stove, then cover and transfer to an oven preheated to 140°C and cook for five to six hours until the meat is very tender.

When tender, remove the meat from the pot and strain the liquid into a deep saucepan, discarding the vegetables. Once the meat has cooled slightly remove the string and, retaining the sausage shape, wrap it tightly in cling film. Pierce a few holes in the film to allow excess liquid to escape, then refrigerate. Meanwhile skim any fat that rises to the top of the braising liquid as it reduces to the consistency of a sauce.

To prepare for serving, remove the meat from the cling film and cut into slices approximately 2.5cm thick. Place these in an ovenproof saucepan together with a little of the braising liquid, then put the pan into the oven at 180°C for 15-20 minutes, regularly basting to establish a shiny glaze. This dish is ideally served with whole glazed carrots, roasted shallots, and butternut squash.

Iced sweet corn parfait and chocolate sorbet

Serves 4

For the sweet corn parfait:

250g sweet corn purée

6 egg yolks

1 teaspoon vanilla extract

250g caster sugar

2 leaves gelatine soaked in cold water

150ml water

350g lightly whipped cream

Put the water and sugar in a large saucepan over a high heat: stir well and bring to the boil for one minute. In a round bottom stainless steel bowl mix the stock syrup together with the egg yolks, vanilla extract and gelatine, and whisk vigorously until it reaches peak stage. Continue whisking until the mixture is cool, then add in the sweet corn purée and gently stir together. Finally, fold in the lightly whipped cream.

Pour the mixture into four stainless steel ring moulds 5cm by 6cm and place in the freezer for 4-5 hours.

For the chocolate sorbet:

200g dark chocolate

500ml semi-skimmed milk

A pinch of ground cumin

250g caster sugar

165ml water

The juice and grated zest from one orange

In a deep saucepan bring the milk, water, sugar and cumin to the boil for about a minute. Take off the heat and stir in the chocolate until it has melted: add the orange juice and zest.

Leave to cool, then churn in an ice cream maker and chill in the freezer until needed.

THE SWAN AT STREATLEY

Neil Thrift

Seared seabass with Singapore noodles and fresh langoustines

Serves 4

Ingredients:

4 x 90g seabass steaks

120g pak choi, blanched

Half a lemon

5g butter

Olive oil

For the pasta:

200g strong flour

5 sachets squid ink

1 size 4 egg

2 egg yolks

50ml olive oil

For the noodles:

Grapeseed oil

5g root ginger, finely chopped

5g garlic, crushed

10g red chilli, finely sliced

45g spring onion, sliced

15g coriander, chopped

5g sugar

For the langoustines:

12 langoustine tails

30g butter

5g flat parsley

Half a lemon

Champagne & lime sauce:

300ml dry champagne

300ml fish stock

300ml double cream

60g butter

30g shallots, finely chopped

Juice of 2 limes

Cayenne pepper

Chervil, tarragon, and parsley stalks

Dried squid noodles can be found at good delicatessens and supermarkets. To make them at home, place all the ingredients for the pasta in a blender, add salt and freshly ground pepper, and pulse blend the mix until the ingredients are bound together in a firm black ball. Wrap this dough in cling film and leave it in the fridge for at least an hour, then unwrap and divide it into four equal portions. Set the roller on the pasta machine to the widest setting, leaving the noodle attachment off at present, and by hand shape the first of the pasta pieces into a rectangle. Cover this in plenty of flour to prevent it sticking, also dusting a little over the machine, and push the pasta through the roller at a steady but firm pace. Once through, cover with flour again and repeat. When the pasta has been through the roller twice, reduce the setting by one and repeat the process. Keep on repeating until the required thickness is achieved: generally, this will be the smallest setting on the machine. Now apply the noodle attachment. Carefully and gently feed the pasta through, then leave the strands to dry on a rolling pin to prevent them sticking together. Repeat this process with the remaining three portions of pasta. Blanch the noodles in boiling salted water for two minutes, refresh in cold water, cover, and set aside.

To prepare the sauce, melt 15g of the butter over a medium heat in a heavy based pan; as it melts add the shallots, cooking slowly without colour until soft. Add 250ml of the champagne and reduce by two thirds, then add the fish stock and reduce by two thirds again. Finally, add the double cream and bring the sauce to the boil, then take it off the heat. Add half the lime juice and herb stalks, season with salt and Cayenne pepper, and leave for 20 minutes. Strain through a fine sieve, leave to cool, and cover.

Heat a non stick frying pan, meanwhile making three small incisions across the skin of the seabass fillets. Put a little olive oil in the pan

and when smoking add the fish, skin side down. Drop in a small knob of butter and season the fillets; when the skins are a crisp golden brown turn the fish and remove the pan from the heat, squeezing a little lemon juice over each fillet. Once the fish is cooked through, remove it from the pan and set aside in a warm place.

Prepare the noodles by heating a wok style pan until smoking, then add the oil, ginger, and garlic, stirring to ensure they don't burn. Add the chilli and sugar (to neutralise the heat from the chilli), then the blanched squid noodles. Stir well and season, then add the spring onion and coriander, cover, and set aside to keep warm.

Heat a separate pan, add the 30g of butter for the langoustines and allow it to froth, then add the langoustine tails and season. Cook until golden brown, then squeeze over the lemon juice and add the parsley.

To assemble, reheat the blanched pak choi in boiling salted water, drain, brush with a little melted butter and keep warm. Warm the champagne and lime sauce and froth with a hand blender, adding in the remaining champagne, lime juice, and butter. Serve as shown: a little oyster sauce – any commercial brand – drizzled around the noodles adds colour and enhances the oriental flavour.

Tian of lamb with red wine butter sauce

Serves 4

All the elements of this dish can be prepared in advance

4 x 180g cannons of lamb

Marinade:

50ml olive oil

15g crushed garlic

5g rosemary

5g thyme

2g black pepper

Anna potatoes:

4 Maris Piper potatoes

30g melted clarified butter

Salt & freshly ground pepper

60g butter

For the sauce:

15g butter

60g chopped shallots

5g thyme leaves

5g rosemary

500ml red wine

250ml port

100ml veal gravy

375g butter, cold, in small cubes

Ratatouille:

50ml olive oil

10g crushed garlic

90g onion/shallot

90g courgette

90g red pepper

90g green pepper

90g aubergine

5g basil, roughly shredded

*90g tomato,
blanched, peeled, deseeded*

Garnish:

20ml olive oil

12 cherry tomatoes

12 cloves garlic, skin on

240g cooked spinach leaves

Ask your butcher for larder trimmed cannons at around 180g each with all the fat and silver sinew removed. Mix the marinade and marinate the meat under cover overnight in the fridge.

To prepare the potatoes, peel and wash them quickly under the tap – don't soak them in water – then take a 3.5cm cutter and cut them lengthwise into four cylinders. Slice these horizontally to a thickness of around 2.5mm and place the discs in a bowl with the clarified butter, mixing well and seasoning. Set out a flat pan and four 7-8cm rings: lay out the potato discs in a circular pattern, each disc overlapping its neighbour, inside the rings until all four have a base of potato. Drizzle olive oil around the outside of the rings and place the pan over a moderate heat. Divide the butter into four and place a piece in the centre of each ring, keeping the heat sufficient to give movement in the pan but not burn the potatoes. When the outsides turn golden brown turn the rings over. Once the rings are browned on both sides, put the pan in the oven at 150°C until thoroughly cooked – around 15 minutes – then leave the potatoes to cool under a light weight. When cooled, remove the potato discs from the pan, setting them out on a tray and covering until needed.

For the ratatouille heat half the olive oil in a flat-bottomed pan. When the oil is hot, cook the onions or shallots and garlic until soft, then remove them from the pan and set aside to cool. In a little more of the oil fry off the courgette, cooking until al dente, then remove from the pan; repeat with the peppers, aubergine and tomato, cooking the last until it starts to break down. When all the ingredients are cooled, mix them together with the basil and cover.

To make the sauce, cook the shallots with the herbs in butter until they are soft but with no colour. Add the alcohol and reduce by nine tenths, then add the veal gravy and bring the liquid back to the boil, reducing by a further two thirds. Check the seasoning. Whisk in the butter a little at a time immediately prior to serving.

Prepare the garnish by frying the cloves of garlic for one to two minutes in oil in a flat bottomed pan, then roasting in the oven at 180°C for about ten minutes until the insides are soft. Add the cherry tomatoes to roast for five minutes, then remove both from the pan and leave to cool.

Remove the lamb from the fridge an hour before cooking. Preheat the oven to 180°C; meanwhile heat up a frying pan and, when smoking, add a little of the oil from the marinade. Season the lamb with salt and pepper and seal until golden brown on both sides. Transfer the lamb to the oven, roasting for eight to ten minutes depending on the degree of cooking preferred; start reheating all the other elements of the dish, either in the oven or on the hob. When cooked, remove the lamb from the oven and keep warm. Using the rings for the Anna potatoes, build up the base of the dish as shown – a layer of spinach leaves, topped by the potatoes, topped with ratatouille – with three cherry tomatoes and garlic cloves on each plate. When the lamb has rested, carve it into slices and arrange these on top of the ratatouille. Pour the sauce around the dish, and serve.

Chocolate passion surprise

Serves 8

Sablée pastry:

600g butter

300g ground almonds

300g icing sugar

2g salt

2g baking powder

100g egg yolks

650g sieved soft flour

Lightly cream the butter, icing sugar, almonds and salt together to make a smooth paste. Add the eggs, baking powder, and soft flour, and continue to blend until the mix returns to a paste: avoid over beating. Leave the paste wrapped in cling film to rest overnight in the fridge, then roll it out to a thickness of 3mm and cut out with a 10cm plain cutter. Transfer the pastry discs to a baking tray and bake for 12-15 minutes at 160°C until done.

Passion chocolate cream:

320g cream

700g passion fruit flesh

600g best quality chocolate

140g butter

Finely chop the chocolate; meanwhile bring the passion fruit to the boil in its own juice and reduce by a third, then add the cream and reduce by a third once more. Pour the hot liquid through a fine sieve over the chocolate and mix with a spatula until all the chocolate has melted. When it is at blood heat (40°C), blend in the cold diced butter, then pour the mixture into 9cm rings and leave to set in the fridge for four hours.

Chocolate sponge:

250g egg whites

80g caster sugar

50g egg yolks

250g chocolate

60g butter

Whisk the egg whites until they form soft peaks, then add the sugar and carry on whisking until it forms high peaks. Heat the chocolate and butter to 40°C, then fold in the meringue with a metal spoon. Pipe the mix into 10cm rings on a baking tray covered with greaseproof paper; bake for around ten minutes at 170°C.

Nougatine:

400g milk

80g glucose

300g sugar

40g butter

2g cardamom powder

100g ground almonds

6g cocoa powder

Boil the milk, sugar, glucose, butter, and cardamom to 105°C, then mix in the cocoa powder and almonds. Pour out the mix onto a baking sheet lined with silicone paper. Spread thinly, and bake for 15-18 minutes at 180°C until fully melted, then remove and leave to harden as it cools.

Poached apricots:

500g dried apricots

Juice of 2 lemons

Black pepper

Halve lengthwise, then place the apricots in a saucepan with a little of the lemon juice and just enough water to cover them. Reduce by half. Add the rest of the lemon juice and pepper to taste, then leave to cool.

Sauce:

1 small tin apricots

1 fresh passion fruit

Orange juice to taste

Blend the tinned apricots with the passion fruit until smooth, adding orange juice to taste and to control the consistency.

To assemble the dish, begin with a foundation of sablée pastry, followed by a layer of chocolate sponge with another layer above of chocolate passion cream into which small chunks of the broken nougatine have been mixed. Top with the poached apricots and a chocolate decoration of your choice; arrange squares of nougatine around the central tower and pour a little of the sauce around the plate.

THE THATCHED COTTAGE HOTEL & RESTAURANT

Martin Matysik

Lobster and avocado salad japonaise

Serves 4

Ingredients:

4 king-sized fresh scallops

1 lobster tail, removed from the shell

1 ripe avocado, peeled and stoned

2 tablespoons chopped fresh tarragon

Juice of $1/2$ lemon

Cayenne pepper

20g Sevruga caviar (optional)

12 pieces of skinned, deseeded ripe tomato, cut into diamond shapes

Sprigs of assorted herbs, plus a few edible flowers such as nasturtiums or chive flowers, to garnish

For the wasabi mayonnaise:

1 teaspoon wasabi paste (Japanese horseradish)

Juice of $1/2$ lemon

1 teaspoon groundnut oil

2 tablespoons mayonnaise

To make the wasabi mayonnaise, mix together the wasabi paste, lemon juice and groundnut oil and stir in the mayonnaise.

Remove and discard the corals from the scallops. Blanch the scallops in boiling water for 30 seconds, then drain, refresh in cold water and drain again. Cut the scallops, lobster meat and avocado into 'brunoise' (tiny dice) and mix with the tarragon. Season with the lemon juice, cayenne and salt, then gently fold in enough wasabi mayonnaise to bind the mixture. Fold in the caviar, if using.

Place 3 heaped dessertspoons of the lobster salad on each serving plate and put a piece of tomato on top of each one. Lightly sprinkle cayenne pepper around the rim of the plate and pour a ribbon of wasabi mayonnaise around the salad. Garnish each plate with a small bouquet of herbs and edible flowers.

Guinness marinated tenderloin of Angus beef with basil mashed potatoes

Serves 4

Ingredients:

800g fillet of Angus beef, certified

200ml balsamic vinegar

300ml red wine

250g brown sugar

1 pint Guinness

300ml groundnut oil

1 bay leaf

200g pesto

600g potato, mashed

2 onions, sliced into rings

150ml milk

50g flour

12 cherry tomatoes

12 slices courgette

Half an onion, chopped

3 cloves of garlic, chopped

200ml olive oil

200g Parmesan

20g flour

1 teaspoon red peppercorns

Trim the beef to remove any tendons and cut into medallions allowing 180g per serving. Prepare the marinade for the beef by bringing the balsamic vinegar, red wine, brown sugar, bay leaf and pepper to the boil in a saucepan, then set aside to cool. When lukewarm, whisk in the Guinness and groundnut oil. Marinate the individual medallions of beef for between 24 and 48 hours.

Good quality ready made pesto is widely available; alternatively make your own using fresh basil and roasted pine nuts with grated Parmesan, olive oil, salt and pepper. Adjust the balance to suit your preference. The pesto will be folded into the mashed potato shortly before serving.

Use the sliced onions to make fried onion rings. Place the cut rings in milk to soften the onion's flavour, drain, then coat in flour and deep fry until golden and crisp.

To prepare the cherry tomatoes and courgette slices, briskly blanch and refresh both in iced water, then peel the tomatoes. Add the chopped onion and garlic, season with salt and pepper and cover with olive oil.

For the Parmesan chips, grate the cheese and sprinkle with flour and red peppercorns. On a baking sheet arrange into small piles and bake at 200°C for around 6 minutes or until crisp and golden.

To cook the beef, season the marinated medallions and pan fry on all sides over a high heat to form a dark crust, then place in the oven until cooked through to your liking. Set the meat aside to rest for about ten minutes. In an earthenware dish, grill the tomato and courgette mix for about three minutes.

To serve, place a large spoonful of basil mash on each plate, then slice the meat and arrange it on top of the potato. Place three further spoons of mash around the meat, each speared with a Parmesan chip. Augment with the flavoured tomato and courgette.

Balsamic beef tea: this translucent sauce with deep and lingering flavours is made by placing the lean meat trimmings in a sealed container without water and cooking in a bain marie. Add the resulting concentrate to a reduction of balsamic vinegar, red wine, and honey.

Cappuccino ice-cream parfait

Serves 4

Ingredients:

1 small egg

2 egg yolks

75g caster sugar

1 gelatine leaf

1 tablespoon Moka liqueur

1 tablespoon Tia Maria

1 teaspoon instant coffee granules

*250ml whipping cream,
plus whipped cream to decorate*

25g marzipan

Ground cinnamon for dusting

For the meringue:

4 egg whites

200g caster sugar

Put the egg, egg yolks and caster sugar in a large bowl set over a pan of barely simmering water, making sure the water is not touching the base of the bowl. Beat with a hand-held electric mixer until the mixture leaves a ribbon on the surface when trailed from the whisk.

Soak the gelatine in cold water for 5 minutes, until softened, then drain. Put it in a small pan with the Moka, Tia Maria and coffee. Heat gently until the gelatine has melted and the coffee has dissolved, then fold it into the egg mixture. Put the bowl in a larger bowl containing ice and leave to cool, taking care not to let it become too stiff. Whisk the cream until it forms soft peaks, then fold it into the mixture. Pour into dairiole moulds, cover with clingfilm

and freeze until set (at least 4 hours).

To make the meringue, whisk the egg whites until they form soft peaks, then whisk in the sugar a little at a time. Continue to whisk until the meringue is stiff and glossy. Put the meringue in a piping bag and pipe coffee saucers and handles on to baking sheets lined with baking parchment. Bake in a very low oven (about 80°C) for 2 hours, until they set hard. Meanwhile, roll out the marzipan into a thin sheet, cut out four 3 x 5cm rectangles and roll

each one up to form an edible cinnamon stick. Sprinkle with ground cinnamon and bake in the oven with the meringues until dry.

To assemble the cappuccino, remove the parfaits from the dairiole moulds by dipping them in hot water and then turning them out. Place each parfait on a meringue saucer, attach the handle at the side and then top with the whipped cream and a dusting of cinnamon. Add the marzipan stick and serve.

John Campbell

Terrine of free range chicken and foie gras

Makes 10 portions

Some say a kitchen can be judged on its terrine as there are so many different cooking techniques involved. This recipe has been developing over the three years of trying to perfect the taste and presentation: it may well be another three years before I'm truly happy with it.

Ingredients:

700g lobe of foie gras

3x 1.2kg free range chickens, legs removed

2 savoy cabbages

4 globe artichokes, cooked in acidulated water, choke removed and cooking liquor retained

20 medium shiitake mushrooms

100g black trompette or other wild mushrooms

200g semi-dried grapes

300ml lamb jus

3 cloves garlic

4 sprigs thyme

200ml duck or goose fat

100g dried haricot blanc – or similar beans – soaked overnight

12 thin slices Parma ham

300ml corn oil

Le Creuset number 21 mould

Preparation

Place the foie gras on an upturned bowl covered with a damp tea towel and leave it at room temperature for 2 hours to bring it to a workable temperature. The liver should open under its own weight to give two sides to the lobe and reveal some blood vessels, fat, and sinew.

Preheat the oven to 180°C. Place a frying pan on the stove and heat about 50ml of corn oil, then take the 3 chicken crowns, season well, and fry them one at a time until sealed and golden all over. Transfer all three to a baking tray and roast for 18-20 minutes until cooked through. Remove from the oven and leave to cool breast down so that the juices run into the breast. Turn the oven down to 60°C for the foie gras.

Bring a large pan of water with a handful of salt to the boil. Prepare a bath of iced water. Discard any damaged or very thick leaves from the cabbage, then remove about two further layers of leaves from each. Trim

Preparation *continued*

off the central branch, leaving two tender sides, then cook for two minutes in the boiling water and plunge into the iced water to arrest cooking. Shape the leaves to give a rectangular piece, then set aside.

Cook the soaked beans in a pan of salted soft water or still bottled water for 45-50 minutes at a very gentle simmer. When they are soft and tender, drain the beans and refresh them in cold water then store in a covered container until needed.

Warm the lamb jus in a small saucepan, At the same time, place a large frying pan over a high heat and add 150ml of corn oil. Lay in the shiitake, tops down, plus the garlic and thyme. Allow the mushrooms to cook for 1-2 minutes, then add the white wine, warm lamb jus, and the rest of the prepared mushrooms. Bring to the boil, then remove from the heat and let the mushrooms cool in the sauce.

Lay out a sheet of cling film and carefully place the soft and open foie gras onto it. With a small sharp knife, remove the main artery that divides the two halves of the lobe, then carefully ease out the rest of the veins. Cut the foie gras into 2" strips, cover with cling film and store in a cool place.

Assembling the terrine

On a work surface, create a double layer of cling film measuring around 30 x 45cm. Use this to line the terrine mould, expelling all the air. Working with the ingredients at just above room temperature ensures that they can be pressed effectively and will absorb other flavours in the terrine. Have a large metal tray close at hand to hold the ingredients as you work with them.

Remove the chicken breasts from the bone and trim off any fat, sinew, and skin. Cut each breast into three lengthways and place in the tray. Strain off the mushrooms, discarding the garlic and thyme but retaining the cooking liquor. Place the mushrooms on the tray.

If cold, warm the artichokes in the retained liquor then slice in half and place on the tray together with the beans, cabbage leaves and semi-dried grapes. In a small pan, heat the duck/goose fat until just melted, then pour it over the ingredients in the tray and season well.

Lay the foie gras on a baking tray lined with kitchen tissue, ensuring a space is left between each piece. Place the tray in the low oven (60°C) for 8 minutes, then remove and set aside.

How the terrine is built is up to you, but two rules must be obeyed. Firstly, strips of cabbage to the exact width of the terrine must be placed at the base and at the top. Secondly, each layer must be brushed with the lamb jus. Otherwise, simply layer the ingredients until they rise to about 2.5cm above the lip of the mould, then arrange the final layer of

cabbage, fold over the lining, and make a tight-fitting seal.

Wrap the whole assembly in another piece of plastic, then with a sharp knife make small incisions about 1cm apart along the edge of the plastic to allow excess juices to escape during pressing. Place a

weight of about 1kg that completely covers the top of the mould to press down the terrine. Place in the fridge with a tray to catch the juices.

Ensure the weight is level and stable, then leave overnight. Carefully unwrap the terrine the following day, trimming to square off the sides. Lay out six pieces of Parma ham on cling film, then carefully sit the terrine on them: lay the other six pieces of ham on top, then press the ham against the terrine and wrap the cling film tightly round. Store for 2-3 days to ensure the maximum infusion of flavour.

When serving, remove from the fridge and slice straight onto the plate. Be sure to allow a few minutes for the terrine to come up to room temperature, as the flavour will be trapped in if it is too cold.

Rabbit saddle, risotto of pea

Serves 6

Ingredients:

3 long saddles of rabbit, boned out and left in one piece with livers retained

150g spinach leaves

6 thin slices of Parma ham

For the risotto:

400g cooked risotto

200g cooked fresh peas

200ml vegetable stock

100g butter

50g Parmesan, grated

For the lentil sauce:

90g cooked Umbri or Puy lentils

3 plum tomatoes, blanched, deseeded, and cut into small dice

300ml strong game or chicken stock

40g cold butter, diced

Sherry vinegar, to taste

1 teaspoon chives, chopped

To garnish:

100g wild mushrooms

100g salsify, cooked

A good handful of spinach

18 button onions, cooked

Split the two natural halves of the rabbit livers with a sharp knife, keeping them as whole as possible, and wrap them in spinach leaves. Trim off any excess fat from the belly flaps of the rabbits and place the wrapped livers in the cavities of the rabbits. On a square sheet of kitchen foil, lay two pieces of Parma ham and place a rabbit saddle on it with the cavity facing up. Roll into a sausage shape, twisting the ends of the foil to ensure a tight seal. Repeat with the other two rabbits and place in the fridge to rest overnight.

To finish the risotto, heat the stock and place the cooked rice in a heavy pan on the stove. Add the hot stock and butter: the amount of stock required is approximate and more should be added if the risotto becomes dry or thick. Bring in the wild mushroom and cooked peas and allow to cook for a further minute, then add the cheese and the risotto is ready to be served.

Preparation of the risotto needs to be timed to completion of the rabbit, for which preheat the oven to 180˚C and roast the rabbit parcels on a baking tray for 17 minutes, turning after 10 minutes. After removal from the oven rest the rabbit in the foil for 3-4 minutes.

Meanwhile, warm the garnish and reduce the game stock. To finish the sauce, add the butter to the reduced stock and whisk to an emulsion, then add the lentils, tomato, and chives, and adjust the seasoning. Finish the sauce with sherry vinegar so that the acidity is just discernible. Arrange and garnish the plate as desired.

Chocolate fondant

Serves 8

Ingredients:

320g dark chocolate

50g butter

50g egg whites

70g sugar

150g egg whites

20g flour t45

Melt the chocolate and butter in a large bowl over a pan of warm water; not too hot or the chocolate will cook. Separately whisk the 50g of egg white with the sugar until it has emulsified but is not aerated. Slowly whisk in the 150g of egg whites until combined, but once again not aerated.

Fold the melted chocolate and butter into the mix, fold in the flour, then immediately pipe into moulds. Allow to rest for two hours in the fridge, then cook at 180°C for 8 minutes: remove, and allow two minutes for resting, then serve with the ice cream of your choice.

WINTERINGHAM FIELDS

Germain Schwab

Foie gras terrine

Makes 16 portions

Ingredients:

500g lobe of foie gras

Duck fat

Demerara sugar

Poire William schnapps

Salt & pepper

For the aspic glaze:

2 leaves gelatine

2 pears, finely chopped

75g demerara sugar

2 sachets squid ink

5g hard licorice

100ml balsamic vinegar

200ml chicken stock

Cook the foie gras very slowly at 56°C for 35 minutes in just enough of the duck fat to cover the lobe. Remove the foie gras from the pan and drain off all excess fat, then de-vein, season with salt and pepper, lightly scatter with demerara sugar, and sprinkle with a little Poire William schnapps. Line a terrine mould with cling film and press the foie gras into the mould, leaving for 24 hours to set.

To prepare the aspic, put the gelatine leaves to one side to soak in cold water. Bring the balsamic vinegar, licorice, chicken stock, squid ink and chopped pears to boil together in a saucepan, then liquidise for one minute. Remove and drain the softened gelatine leaves, add them to the liquid and allow the gelatine to dissolve.

Turn out the foie gras terrine onto a cooling rack, gently spoon over the aspic until it starts to coat the surface, then completely cover the terrine. Leave to set in the fridge for a couple of hours. When ready, slice thinly with a sprinkle of sea salt on each slice, and serve with toasted brioche or with pan fried foie gras on brioche with spiced pear chutney as shown.

Lovage pasta nest with Avruga caviar sauce

Serves 6

Ingredients:

25g Avruga caviar

500g pasta flour

200g lovage leaves

3 whole eggs

3 egg yolks

2 soup spoons olive oil

750ml fish stock for sauce

Boil the lovage for two minutes, remove and refresh in cold water, then liquidise with a little boiling water. Measure 100ml of this purée for use in the recipe.

Pour the flour into a blender. In a separate bowl, mix the eggs, purée and olive oil to a smooth liquid: turn on the blender and add the liquid a little at a time until it is smooth but not sticky. Rest the dough for twenty minutes, then divide up into six equal portions. Roll each portion in a pasta machine, from #8 to #1, then run the sheet of pasta through the tagliatelle attachment. Drape the strands around a rolling pin to prevent them sticking together for an hour.

Prepare a sauce using 750ml of fish stock; when it has reduced by two thirds and reached a good consistency gently fold in the caviar. Place the pasta in salted boiling water for 15 seconds, strain and serve, spooning the caviar mixture around a 'nest' of pasta twirled with a fork.

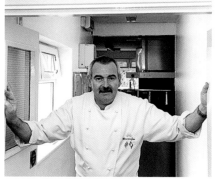

Fruit jellies

Ingredients:

500g fruit purée (citrus are excellent)

75g glucose sugar

600g caster sugar

7 leaves gelatine

Place your chosen fruit in a blender to make a smooth purée for the jellies. Insert all the ingredients apart from the gelatine in a pan and bring to the boil: reduce for five minutes, then bring to 100°C - 110°C, skimming off any foam or other residue on the surface. Take off the heat and dissolve the gelatine leaves in the liquid.

Pour the cooled liquid into buttered shallow trays (around 2cm deep), and leave to set for two to three days: this gives time for the jellies to properly dry out. Cut into squares and roll the cubes in icing sugar. Keep in an airtight container, but not in the fridge.

THE WORDSWORTH HOTEL

Bernard Warne

Assiette of duck

Serves 8

Shallot tatin with foie gras:

200g shallots, finely diced

200ml red wine

100ml red wine vinegar

1 teaspoon redcurrant jelly

1 sprig of thyme

200g foie gras

8 x 5cm puff pastry discs

Heat and reduce the shallots, wine, vinegar, jelly and seasonings to the consistency of jam, then leave to cool. Spread the jam over the pastry discs and bake for ten minutes at 180°C. Cut the foie gras into slices, then sauté until browned on both sides: use to top the tatins.

Duck confit & apple terrine:

6-8 duck legs

1 litre duck fat

75g sea salt

1 bouquet garni (in muslin)

2 Granny Smith apples

25g butter

10g sugar

Rub the duck legs with salt and leave for two hours, then wipe off the salt and add to the rest of the ingredients in a heavy based pan. Cook gently for two to three hours – the slower the better – until the meat is coming off the bone, then drain off and set aside the fat. Shred the meat from the bones with two forks, adding a little of the fat to keep the meat moist.

Peel, quarter and slice the apples, then sprinkle the slices with sugar and cook in the butter until caramelised but not soft. Mix with the duck meat, reserving 150g of the confit for the duck samosa, then gently press into a terrine mould lined with cling film and leave to set overnight in the fridge. Serve cold, preferably with a sweated julienne of leek in a sherry and walnut oil vinaigrette.

Spiced duck samosa:

A fine dice of 1 small chilli,
$1/2$ small onion, 1 garlic clove

50g carrot

50g celery

50g courgette

1 tablespoon chopped coriander leaf

1 teaspoon grated ginger

Splash of kecap manis

150g duck confit (see above)

50g butter

Salt & pepper

8 squares Chinese spring roll pastry

Sweat down the dice in the butter, then add the rest of the vegetables finely chopped: cook lightly, then stir in the coriander, ginger, kecap manis and confit. When heated through, divide onto the squares of pastry, halved diagonally and sealed to make samosas. Deep fry until the pastry is crisp and brown: serve with beetroot chutney.

Seared duck breast with plums:

1 x 300g Magret duck breast

100ml port

4 Victoria plums

Season and sear the duck breast, then set aside to rest. Add the port to the pan and reduce by two thirds, then lower the heat and add the sliced plums, gently warming them through. Slice the breast into eight and serve on the plums with the jus.

Smoked duck breast with orange:

1 x 250g smoked duck breast, thinly sliced

8 segments orange

Juice of 2 oranges

1 sprig lemon thyme

5ml groundnut oil

100g fine green beans

Reduce the orange juice with the lemon thyme until syrupy then leave to cool, gently stirring in the oil to emulsify the liquid. Blanch and refresh the beans and cut into 3cm lengths, then arrange on the plate and dress with the orange sauce, topped by sliced breast and a segment of orange.

Roulade of chicken with spring onion, sunblush tomatoes and feta cheese

Serves 4

For the mousse:

3 chicken fillets

1 egg

1 egg yolk

250g whipping cream

1 teaspoon truffle oil

For the roulade:

3 chicken breasts

3 sheets sushi nori

For the potato tuile:

125g mashed potato, passed

2 egg whites

2 tablespoons clarified butter

Herb purée

For the tomato & feta cheese mix:

4 sunblush tomatoes, diced

4 plum tomatoes, concassé

110g feta cheese

2 spring onions, diced

Blend the ingredients for the mousse together until smooth and rest in the fridge. With a sharp knife open out the chicken breasts and flatten the meat with a tenderiser until it is very thin. Butter a sheet of 35 x 25cm greaseproof paper, then lay out the thin chicken meat and season. Spread the mousse in a thin layer over the meat and top with the nori. Roll like a Swiss roll (removing from the paper) and wrap the cylinder tightly in cling film: refrigerate for at least an hour.

Reheat the refined mashed potato in a pan with the rest of the ingredients until they are fully combined, then leave to cool in the fridge for half an hour. To make the tuiles spread and shape the paste on silicone paper and dry out in a very low oven. Store under airtight conditions if not immediately required.

When ready to serve, divide the roulade into four equal portions while it is still wrapped in the film. Sear both ends, then remove the film and cook in the oven for 10 – 15 minutes at 180°C. Rest, keeping warm, meanwhile quickly sauté together the ingredients for the tomato and cheese mix. Plate the tomato mix using a ring as a guide, with the roulade on top. Shown here served with aubergine tapenade, small fondant potatoes, chicken jus, and the potato tuile.

Dark chocolate mousse with Griottine cherries

Makes 8 portions

Ingredients:

225g dark chocolate

25ml milk

25ml Griottine cherry liqueur

16 Griottine cherries

50g pasteurised egg whites

60ml whipping cream

25g caster sugar

8 x 5cm chocolate sponge discs

Line eight 5cm rings with acetate strips, then place a sponge disc and two of the cherries in the base of each. Gently melt the chocolate with the milk and liqueur, then leave to cool: fold in the whipped cream, the whisked egg whites, and the sugar. Pipe the mix into the rings and leave in the fridge to set for at least four hours.

Shown served with a white chocolate ice cream, an almond tuile ring and cherry sauce.

CONTACT INFORMATION

12
BAILIFFSCOURT HOTEL

CLIMPING
WEST SUSSEX BN17 5RW

01903 723511

17
BALLYNAHINCH CASTLE

BALLYNAHINCH
RECESS, CONNEMARA
CO. GALWAY
IRELAND

00 353 9531006

22
BLAKES HOTEL

33 ROLAND GARDENS
LONDON SW7 3PF

020 7370 6701

31
CALLOW HALL

MAPPLETON ROAD
NEAR ASHBOURNE
DERBYSHIRE DE6 2AA

01335 300900

36
CASHEL PALACE

MAIN STREET
CASHEL, CO. TIPPERARY
IRELAND

00 353 62 62707

42
**CHARLTON HOUSE
& THE MULBERRY RESTAURANT**

CHARLTON ROAD
SHEPTON MALLET
SOMERSET BA4 4PR

01749 342008

47
CHEWTON GLEN

NEW MILTON
HAMPSHIRE BH25 6QS

01425 275341

52
CHILSTON PARK

SANDWAY
LENGHAM, MAIDSTONE
KENT ME17 2BE

01622 859803

26
CITY CAFE RESTAURANT, BAR & TERRACE
BIRMINGHAM

1 BRUNSWICK SQUARE
BRINDLEYPLACE
BIRMINGHAM B1 2HW

0121 643 1003

58
CITY CAFE RESTAURANT, BAR & TERRACE
BRISTOL

TEMPLE ROSE STREET
TEMPLE WAY
BRISTOL BS1 6BF

0117 9251001

INDEX
OF DISHES

Melon: rosettes with mango, prosciutto, and chilli salsa 76

Mixed summer berries with a warm red wine and orange juice flavoured with cinnamon 112

Monkfish: medallions wrapped in smoked salmon 39

Noisettes of lamb with a spaghetti of vegetables and garlic and thyme jus 48

Paella of seabass and scallops 176

Pan fried halibut, baby asparagus, and saffron butter 18

Pan-fried scallops on roasted asparagus with chive butter sauce 199

Pandan pudding with blueberry compote 25

Passion fruit jelly with coconut sorbet, pineapple fritters 192

Peach melba 180

Pear mousse in a chocolate cup, Poire William sabayon 174

Pineapple:

    caramelised honey and chilli 149

    carpaccio with nougat glace 90

    fritters 192

Poached lobster with basil custard 189

Pork:

    fillet roasted in Parma ham 33

    honey roast belly 42

Pressed tomato timbale, goats cheese and basil fondant and 25 year old balsamic vinegar 104

Quail:

    breast with red chard and black pudding 160

    roast on fondant potato with wild mushroom and Madeira sauce 200

    roast quail breast on a cabbage confit 167

    warm terrine with black pudding and foie gras 118

Rabbit and walnut salad with orange dressing 98

Rabbit saddle, risotto of pea 240

Rabbit:

    and walnut salad with orange dressing 98

    duo with root vegetables 78

    stuffed saddle with basil 126

    stuffed saddle with mustard and herbs 42

Raspberry and shortbread millefeuille with bittersweet chocolate sorbet 34

Raspberry millefeuille with mandarin sorbet 186

Ravioli of caramelised Autumn root vegetables, plum tomato fondue, cappucino of bay leaf 205

Red mullet: marinated with Provençal vegetables 53

Risotto dumplings of smoked trout and smoked haddock 93

Risotto:

    lobster and pearl barley 165

    lobster and soft herb 163

    mushroom 39

    pea 240

    spiced butternut squash 156

Roast breast of grouse with sweetcorn purée 86

Roast fillet of turbot, soft herb and lobster risotto, curry oil and aged balsamico 163

Roast lobster with orange and sesame dressing 140

Roast lobster wrapped in pancetta with a haricot bean and truffle fricassée 55

Roast peach with lemon crème caramel 84

Roast quail breast on a cabbage confit with crisp potato galette, surrounded by lightly cooked wild fungi 167

Roast quail on fondant potato with wild mushroom and Madeira sauce 200

Roast rack of Cornish lamb with black truffle potatoes 29

Roast saddle of venison with braised cos, celeriac, baby leek, and bitter chocolate sauce 206

Roast seabass with a ravioli of langoustine and amaretto, shellfish sauce and saffron oil 145

Roasted breast of duck, confit of leg, fricassée of baby vegetables, orange sauce 14

Roasted cod and braised beef 101

Roasted fillet of barramundi, cassoulet of beans and purple potato, sauce Jacqueline 119

Roasted scallops and John Dory with langoustines, truffle pomme purée, black and white puddings and Madeira sauce 105

Roe deer: canon with potato, black pudding and shallot torte 136

Rosettes of seasonal melon with mango, prosciutto, and chilli salsa 76

Roulade of chicken with spring onion, sunblush tomatoes and feta cheese 253

Salad of Cornish lobster with avocado and mango 130

Salad of duck and langoustine 47

Salmon ceviche, avocado ice cream and oyster beignets 155

Salmon terrine with white bean dressing 139

Salmon: tian of cured salmon & crab 109

Scallops:

    paella with seabass 176

    pan-fried on roasted asparagus 199

    roasted with John Dory and langoustines 105

    seared with beetroot crème fraîche 36

    seared with beetroot jam 26

    seared with parsnip purée 12

    seared with sweet peppers 17

    seared with tomato tian 183

Scottish langoustines with sweet spices and a light fennel bavarois 194

Scrambled eggs with cockles and roasted peppers 81

Sea bass:

    baked with crispy fennel skin 23

    on basil crushed potato with aubergine and courgette 45

The King and I